The Essentials of Project Management

Second Edition

Dennis Lock

Gower

First published 1996

This edition published by
Gower Publishing Limited
Gower House
Croft Road
Aldershot
Hampshire GU11 3HR
England

Gower Publishing Company
131 Main Street
Burlington VT 05401-5600 USA

Dennis Lock has asserted his right under the Copyright, Designs and Patents Act 1988 to be identified as the author of this work.

British Library Cataloguing in Publication Data
Lock, Dennis 1929–
    The essentials of project management. – 2nd ed.
    1. Industrial project management
    I. Title
    658. 4'04

ISBN 0 566 08224 1

Library of Congress Cataloging-in-Publication Data
Lock, Dennis.
    The essentials of project management / Dennis Lock.– 2nd ed.
        p. cm.
    ISBN 0-566-08224-1 (pbk)
    1. Industrial project management.   I. Title.

T56.8 I57 2000
658.4'04–dc21   99-057306

Typeset in Palatino by IML Typographers, Chester and printed in Great Britain by MPG Books Ltd, Bodmin

Contents

Functional matrix organizations – Variations of the
matrix organization – Project team organization – Which
type of organization is best? – The hybrid option –
Organizations with more than one project manager
– The project manager himself – Project services groups

List of figures

Preface

The origins of this book lie in my larger and long-established work *Project Management*. That book has grown steadily in size and scope since its first appearance in 1968 and its sixth edition reached 24 chapters where the first had only nine. Its readership has included many tens of thousands of managers and senior students of project management.

People other than professional project managers will, at some time in their lives, be faced with the need to manage at least one project. Perhaps you will have to set up a market research project for your company or arrange an exhibition or other event. Occasional projects might include anything from managing the relocation of a company to organizing a pop festival, from choosing and installing a complex new computer system to conducting a school outward bound expedition, from a do-it-yourself building project to running an election campaign.

Most new ventures falling into this 'occasional project' category can benefit enormously from proven project management ideas and methods; it is not only the large industrial projects that need careful organization, planning and control. But not everyone called upon to manage a project will have the time or need to study a work as comprehensive as *Project Management*. Where, then, can the managers of small or occasional projects look to acquire the key skills? Thus the need became apparent for a new, smaller book dedicated to just the essentials of project management.

Publication of the first edition of *The Essentials of Project Management* in 1996 produced results that delighted Gower and myself, the high and sustained level of sales indicating that this book had met a real need and a waiting readership. That first edition was compiled almost entirely from carefully distilled extracts of the sixth edition of *Project Management*. When *Project Management* reached its seventh edition, it was an obvious step to review *The Essentials of Project Management* and take advantage of the additions and improvements made to the parent book. This second edition is the result.

The organization of chapters remains unchanged but there are numerous small revisions, one or two corrections and new examples and illustrations. Every one of the 58 illustrations has been scrutinized for clarity and is either completely new or has been redrawn. Significant text changes include an expanded account of project matrix organizations, an introduction to the responsibility matrix chart and a more conventional approach to earned value analysis.

So, welcome to this enhanced edition of *The Essentials of Project Management*. It is my hope that this book will continue its record of service to the managers of all kinds of occasional projects, to students and to anyone who needs a practical introduction to the rewarding pursuit of project management.

Dennis Lock
2001

Acknowledgements

I am indebted to the following companies:

WST Limited for providing Open Plan software
Forgetrack Limited for the provision of Primavera software
Whitaker for access to their Bookbank databases on CD-ROM for
bibliographic research

Microsoft Project, Microsoft Project 98 and MS-DOS are registered
    trademarks and Windows is a trademark of Microsoft Corpora-
    tion.
Open Plan and Open Plan Professional are registered trademarks
    of WST Corporation.
Primavera Project Planner is a registered trademark.

                                                            DL

1

Introduction

Projects and the means for managing them are hardly new, as the wonders of the ancient world testify. However, in recent years project management has become recognized as a branch of management in its own right, with its own professional associations and with a comprehensive and expanding range of procedures and techniques.

The purpose of project management is to plan, organize and control all activity so that the project is completed as successfully as possible in spite of all the difficulties and risks. This process starts before any resources are committed and must continue until all work is finished. The aim is for the final result to satisfy the objectives of both the project performer and the customer.

Most people think of a customer as an individual person or external organization that enters into a sales contract with the project performer. But many projects are conducted internally, within organizations for their own purposes. At the simplest extreme, an individual might wish to carry out a project single-handed for him- or herself. In all these cases there is still a notional customer for the project and appropriate methods must still be used to manage the project if that customer is to be satisfied.

Today's project manager has ready access to a wider than ever range of cost-effective tools for planning and controlling a project. The most successful manager will be capable of choosing and using those techniques that best suit the particular project. But there is obviously far more to managing a project of any significant size than the application of a few sophisticated techniques and procedures. It involves a whole framework of logical and progressive planning and decisions, perceptiveness, the liberal application of common sense, proper organization, effective commercial and financial management, painstaking attention to documentation, and a clear grasp of proven and long-established principles of management and leadership.

Projects

The principal identifying characteristic of any project is its novelty. It is a step into the unknown, fraught with risk and uncertainty. No two projects are ever exactly alike, and even a repeated project will differ from its predecessor in one or more commercial, administrative or physical aspects.

Projects can be classified under four main headings:

1   *Civil engineering, construction, petrochemical, mining and quarrying projects*   These generally involve work on a site which is exposed to the elements, remote from the contractor's head office. Such projects incur special risks and problems of organization and communication. They often require massive capital investment and they deserve (but do not always get) rigorous management of progress, finance and quality. The amount of finance and other resources may be too great for one contractor, in which case the organization and communications are further complicated by the participation of several contractors, working together in some kind of joint venture.

2   *Manufacturing projects,* for new product development or to produce a piece of equipment or machinery, ship, aircraft, land vehicle or some other item of specially designed hardware. Manufacturing projects are often conducted in factories or other home-based environments, where it should be

possible to exercise on-the-spot management and provide an optimum working environment.

3 *Management projects*, which prove the point that every company, whatever its size, can expect to need project management expertise at least once in its lifetime. These are the projects that arise when companies relocate, develop and introduce a new computer system, prepare for a trade exhibition, research and produce a feasibility report, set up a training programme, restructure the organization or plan a spectacular celebration.

4 *Research projects* Projects for pure research can consume vast sums of money, last for many years and either result in a dramatically profitable discovery or prove to have been a complete waste of time and money. Research projects carry very high risk: they aim to extend the boundaries of current knowledge. Their end objectives are usually difficult or impossible to define. However, some form of control must be attempted. Budgets have to be set in line with available funding. Expenditure can be controlled to some extent by conducting regular management reviews and reassessments, and by authorizing and releasing funds in periodic, controlled and carefully considered steps.

Project management processes

The left-hand column of Figure 1.1 lists project management processes that are directly related to planning and controlling most commercial and industrial projects. These are the processes with which this book is chiefly concerned. The seventh edition of my book *Project Management* was the source for practically all the material used in this book. That book is more comprehensive, contains more case studies and includes the additional topics listed in the right-hand column of Figure 1.1.

Principal project management subjects covered in this book	Additional subjects covered in the 7th edition of *Project Management*
• Project objectives • Association for Project Management • Project definition • Project organization • Work breakdown • Coding • Cost estimating • Planning by bar charts • Planning by network analysis • Simple resource scheduling • Computing examples • Project authorization • Implementing project work • Routine project purchasing • Shipping, port and customs formalities • Changes • Progress management • Project closure	• Triangle of objectives • PRINCE 2 • Cost estimating, in greater detail • Financial project appraisal • Contracts • Contract payment structures • Insuring risk • Line of balance for construction projects • Line of balance for manufacturing projects • PERT • Resource scheduling, in greater detail • Cash flow scheduling • Choosing computer software • Computer case studies • Standard networks and templating • Multiproject resource scheduling • Computer program for risk analysis • Purchasing for capital projects • Immediate action orders • Production permits • Manufacturing concessions • Earned value analysis • Project closure, in greater detail

Figure 1.1　The essential processes of project management

Project objectives

The objectives of most projects can be grouped under three headings:

1　Quality

The end result of the project must be fit for the purpose for which it was intended. The specification must be satisfied. If a new copper refinery is designed and built for the purpose of processing 200 000 tonnes of cathode copper per annum, then it must be able to do so, and to produce copper at the rated purity. The plant must function reliably, efficiently and safely. In these enlightened times there will be trouble if operation of the plant causes environmental pollution. Development projects for consumer goods must produce articles that satisfy the market requirements. The design engineering and manufacturing quality have to result in a reliable and safe product.

A management project for the relocation of a company should see a contented workforce at their desks in the new buildings on the appointed day, with all their goods and chattels delivered without loss or damage to the right places, and all company systems operational.

At one time quality was seen primarily as the responsibility of the quality control department, relying on inspection and testing to discover faults and then arranging for their rectification. Now, the concept of total quality management is uppermost, with responsibility for quality shared by everyone in the project organization from top to bottom.

Most of this book is about achieving time and cost objectives. Achieving quality, performance and reliability objectives obviously requires technological competence, but this must be complemented by adequate quality procedures (for which ISO 9000 is accepted as the controlling series of standards and the starting point from which to install and operate a quality management system).

2 Budget

The project must be completed without exceeding the authorized expenditure.

For commercial or industrial projects, failure to complete work within budgeted costs must reduce the profits and any expected return on the capital invested, with risk of actual financial loss.

There are many projects, however, where there is no direct profit motive. Examples include internal management projects, pure scientific research, some charitable works and projects carried out solely by employees of local authorities using public funds. For these projects too, even in the absence of a profit motive, careful attention to cost budgets and financial management is vital.

3   Time to completion

Actual progress has to match or beat planned progress. All significant stages of the project must take place no later than their specified dates, to result in project completion on or before the planned finish date. This timescale objective is extremely important. Late completion or delivery of a commercial project is, to say the least, hardly likely to please the project purchaser or sponsor. Consistently failing to keep delivery promises cannot enhance the contractor's market reputation. Further, any project that continues to use the contracting company's resources beyond its scheduled finish date is liable to have a knock-on effect and disrupt the company's following projects.

The time/cost relationship

'Remember that TIME IS MONEY!'
(Benjamin Franklin, in *Advice to a Young Tradesman*, 1748)

I have always held that the most important aspect of cost control is the management of project time. If the planned timescale is exceeded, the original cost estimates and budgets are almost certain to be exceeded too.

Direct costs

'Variable' or 'direct' project costs are time-related in several ways. Cost inflation is one factor. A project started and finished considerably later than the time originally planned might cost more because of intervening rises in the costs of payroll, materials and bought-out services.

Late working can sometimes be associated with inefficient working, perhaps through lost time or waiting time (often the result of bad organization and planning). If any project task takes longer to perform than its planned duration, there is a risk that the budgeted man-hours will also be exceeded. This is true not only for one task in a project but also collectively for the whole project.

Indirect (overhead) costs

The 'fixed' or 'overhead' costs of management (administration, accommodation, services and general facilities) are directly time-related: they are incurred day by day, every day, regardless of any work actually achieved, until the project is finished. If the project runs late, then these costs will have to be borne for a longer period than planned and must exceed their budget.

Costs of financing

Another important time-related cost is financing. Where the project performer has an overdraft at the bank or relies on other loan financing, interest has to be paid on the loan. Even if the peformer finances the project from its own funds, there is still a notional cost of financing, equivalent to the interest or dividends that the same funds could have earned had they been invested elsewhere. If a project runs late, the financing period is extended, and the amount of interest or notional interest payable must increase correspondingly.

Much of the finance raised for a large industrial project is likely to be invested in work in progress. Work in progress includes not only visible signs of work carried out in a factory or at a construction site; it also includes all the unbilled costs of engineering and design. In many cases the contractor is only able to charge for work actually finished and delivered to the customer, or for amounts of work done and supported by certified invoices. Such invoices are validated by certificates from an independent professional third party (often a quantity surveyor or an engineer) which certify the amount of work done and claimed for. Certified invoices are often linked to planned events. If an event is late, or if a measurable progress stage has not been reached, an invoice cannot be issued.

Contract penalties

Some contracts contain a penalty clause which provides the customer with the sanction of a cost penalty against the contractor if the project should run late. A penalty clause might, for example, specify a sum of money to be deducted from the agreed project price for each week by which the contractor fails to meet the contracted project completion time.

Balancing time, cost and quality

Of course the aim of a good project manager must be to achieve success in all aspects of the project. But it is occasionally necessary to identify one of the three primary objectives (quality, cost or time) as being of special importance. This will affect the priority given to the allocation of scarce resources and the way in which management attention should be concentrated. It might also influence the choice of project organization structure (see Chapter 3).

A project for a charitable organization with very limited funds would, for example, have to be controlled very much with the costs in mind.

Some companies stake everything on their reputation for quality, even if this means overrunning time and costs. However, when quality is mentioned in this context it is actually the *level of specification* that is meant. Quality itself, meaning fitness for purpose, should never be compromised: it is not a negotiable factor. A customer might agree with an architect that a great deal of money could be saved on a new house by substituting carpets for the originally intended marble floors. Those floors must still, however, be capable of giving good service. Fundamental quality and reliability have not been changed because the carpeted floors should still be fit for their main intended purpose. It is the specification that has been downgraded.

A project to set up a stand at a trade exhibition, for which the dates have been announced and the venue booked, is obviously very dependent on meeting the time objective. Such a project might need the establishment of a task force which is given first claim on any common services or other resources. If there is any danger of the project running late, the cost objective becomes secondary because the most important factor is to be at the exhibition when it opens – not the day after it has closed!

The Association for Project Management

The profession of project management is represented by the International Association of Project Management (IPMA). The corporate member of the IPMA in the UK is the Association for Project Management (APM) and further information is available from the secretariat at Thornton House, 150 West Wycombe Road, High Wycombe, Buckinghamshire HP12 3AE.

The Association arranges seminars and meetings through a network of local branches and publishes the monthly journal *Project*. Membership of the Association is a good way for project managers and all others involved in project management to meet and to maintain current awareness of modern techniques, practices and computer systems.

The Association has a well-established certification procedure for project managers, who must already be full members. To quote from the Association's own literature, 'the certificated project manager is at the pinnacle of the profession, possessing extensive knowledge and having carried responsibility for the delivery of at least one significant project'.

2

Definition

Project definition is a process which starts when the customer or investor first conceives the idea of a project. It does not end until the last piece of information has been filed to describe the project in its finished 'as-built' condition. Figure 2.1 shows some of the elements in the process for a project of significant size. This chapter concentrates on that part of project definition which should take place before a project is authorized. This is the process that is essential to setting the project on the correct course and which plays a vital role in establishing the initial contractual commitments.

The customer's project specification

When any company receives an enquiry for new work, the customer's requirements must be clearly established and understood. The project must be defined as well as possible right at the start. The contracting company must know for what it is bidding and what its commitments would be in the event of winning the contract.

Adequate project definition is equally important for the cus-

11

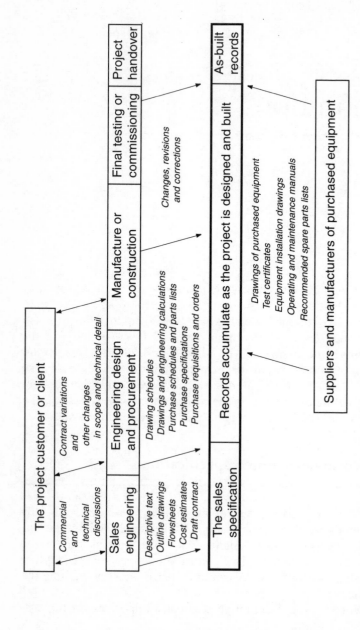

Figure 2.1 The process of project definition

12

tomer, which must be clear on what it expects to get for its money. This point applies just as much to any company considering an in-house project, in which case that company (in the role of project customer) must be clear on what will be the outcome of its investment.

Initial enquiries from customers can take many different forms. Perhaps a set of plans or drawings will be provided, or a written description of the project objectives. A combination of these two, rough sketches or even a verbal request are other possibilities. Ensuing communications between the customer and contractor, both written and verbal, can result in subsequent qualifications, changes or additions to the original request.

All of these elements, taken together and documented, constitute the 'customer specification', to which all aspects of any tender and subsequent contract or purchase order must relate. As with all other types of specifications, the customer's project specification must be identifiable at all times by means of a unique reference number, date and issue or revision number.

Project scope

It is obviously important for the contractor to determine in advance exactly what the customer expects for the money. The requirements must be documented in unambiguous terms, so that they are understood and similarly interpreted by customer and contractor alike. Equally important is the way in which responsibility for the work is to be shared between the contractor, the customer and others. The scope of work required from the contractor, the size of its contribution to the project, must be made clear.

At its simplest, the scope of work required might be limited to making and delivering a piece of hardware in accordance with drawings supplied by the customer. At the other extreme, the scope of a large construction or process plant project could mean that the contractor will handle the project entirely, responsible for all work until the purchaser is able to accept the handover of a fully completed and proven project (known as a turnkey operation).

There is usually a range of ancillary items to be considered. Will the contractor be responsible for training the customer's staff and, if so, how much (if any) training is to be included in the project contract and price? What about commissioning, or support during the first few weeks or months of the project's working life? What sort of warranty or guarantee is going to be expected? Are any training, operating or maintenance instructions to be provided? If so, how many copies and in what language?

Answers to all of these questions must be provided, as part of project definition, before cost estimates, pricing, tenders and binding contracts can be made.

Using checklists

Checklists are a useful way of making certain that nothing important is forgotten. Contractors who have amassed a great deal of experience in their particular field of project operation will learn the types of questions that must be asked of the customer in order to fill in most of the information gaps and arrive at a specification that is sufficiently complete.

The simplest application of a checklist is seen when a sales engineer takes a customer's order for equipment that is standard, but which can be ordered with a range of options. The sales engineer might use a pad of preprinted forms, ticking off the options that the customer wants. People selling replacement windows to householders use such pads. The forms are convenient and help to prevent important details being omitted when the order is taken and passed back to the factory for action.

Companies about to tender for construction, petrochemical or mining projects can make good use of checklists. One checklist might be used to verify that plant performance or building accommodation needs are properly specified. Local climatic and geological data at the intended project site may have to be defined. If the project site is in a foreign country, the contractor may not know about potential hazards such as high winds or earth tremors, and it may also be necessary to check on any special statutory regulations which operate in the region. Other data might cover national working practices and the influence of local trade unions, the availability of suitable local labour, facilities to be provided for the contractor's expatriate staff and so on. Many, many questions will have to be asked and answered.

Checklists are ideal in these circumstances. The example in Figure 2.2 is an extract from a comprehensive project definition checklist used by an international mining company.

The contractor's initial design specification

If after serious consideration of the customer's specification a contractor decides to prepare a tender, the contractor must obviously put forward technical and commercial proposals for carrying out the work. These proposals will also form a basis for the contractor's own design specification. The requirements defined by the customer's specification will usually need to be translated into a form compatible with the contractor's own normal practice, quality standards, technical methods and capabilities. The design specification will provide this link.

The desired end results of a project can often be achieved by a variety of technical or logistical concepts and there could be considerable differences between proposals submitted by companies competing for the same order. Different methods are usually associated with different costs and ease of construction or manufacture, as well as having implications for performance, safety and reliability.

It often happens during proposal considerations that design concepts are discussed and chosen because of their attractive cost implications. These intentions often assume that short cut measures can be taken when the project becomes live, perhaps making use of designs used on earlier projects or which are known to be of cost benefit to the manufacturing or construction departments.

For these reasons it is vital for the successful contractor to document the intended design approach in as much detail as possible when the project proposal is made and to ensure subsequently that the project is built according to those decisions.

Without a detailed design specification, there would be a danger that a project could be costed, priced and sold against one set of design solutions but actually executed using a different,

Project site and other local conditions

Availability of utilities
- Electrical power
- Potable water
- Other water
- Sewerage
- Other services
Transport
- Existing roads
- Access difficulties (low bridges, weight limits, etc.)
- Nearest railpoint
- Nearest suitable seaport
- Nearest commercial airport
- Local airstrip
- Local transport and insurance arrangements
Physical conditions
- Seismic situation
- Temperature range
- Rainfall or other precipitation
- Humidity
- Wind force and direction
- Dust
- Barometric pressure
- Site plans and survey
- Soil investigation and foundation requirements
Local workshop and manufacturing facilities
Local sources of bulk materials
Local plant hire
Site safety and security
Local human resources available
- Professional
- Skilled
- Unskilled
Site accommodation arrangements for:
- Offices
- Secure stores
Site living accommodation for:
- Expatriate managers and engineers
- Artisans
- Short stay visitors
- Married quarters (see separate checklist if these are required)

Figure 2.2   Part of a project definition checklist

Other site facilities
- First aid, medical and hospital facilities
- Catering and messing arrangements
- Hotels or other accommodation for VIPs
- Local banking arrangements

Communications
- General mail and airmail service
- Special mail or courier service
- Telephone over public network
- Telephone over dedicated terrestrial or satellite link
- Fax
- E-mail
- Telex
- Other

Contractual and commercial conditions

How firm are the proposals?
What are the client's relative priorities for:
- Time?
- Cost?
- Quality?

What are the client's delivery requirements?
Do we know the client's budget levels?
Scope of work envisaged:
- Basic design only?
- Fully detailed design?
- Procurement responsibility: ourselves, the client or someone else?
- Construction responsibility: ourselves, the client or a managing contractor?
- Commissioning, customer training, operating and maintenance manuals, etc. (these must be specified)

How accurate are the existing cost estimates:
- Ballpark?
- Comparative?
- Have all estimates been checked against the estimating manual checklist?

How is the project to be financed?
Is there to be a financial guarantor?
What do we know about the client's financial status and invoice payment record?
Are contract penalty clauses expected?
Is the pricing to be firm or other?
What are the likely arrangements for stage or progress payments?
What retention payment will be imposed?
What insurances must we arrange?
What guarantees or warranties will the client expect?

Figure 2.2   *Concluded*

more costly, approach. This danger is very real. It occurs in practice when the period between submitting a quotation and actually receiving the order exceeds a few months, allowing the original intentions to be forgotten.

A specification is intended to do what its name implies: to specify that which shall be done. The manager who allows subordinates to depart without good cause from an agreed design specification is guilty of incompetence or weakness, or both.

Specification of production methods

Similar arguments to those discussed above for design apply to the need to associate the production methods actually used in manufacturing projects with those assumed in the cost estimates and subsequent budgets.

It can happen that certain rather bright individuals make suggestions during the proposal stage for cutting corners and saving expected costs – all aimed at securing a lower and more competitive tender price. That is, of course, laudable. Provided that these ideas are recorded with the estimates, all will be well and the cost savings can be achieved when the project goes ahead.

Now imagine what could happen if a project proposal were to be submitted by one branch of the organization but, when an order is eventually received, the company's managers decide to switch the work to a production facility at another, far away location in the organization. If all the original ideas for saving production costs had not been recorded, the cost consequences could be disastrous. Unfortunately, it is not necessary to transfer work between different locations for mistakes of this kind to arise. Even the resignation of one production engineer from a manufacturing company could produce such consequences if that engineer's intentions had not been adequately recorded.

The golden rule, once again, is to define and document the project in all respects before the estimates are made and translated into budgets and price.

Construction specification

Construction projects offer another example of work that has to be defined by specification. All building contractors of any repute work from detailed specifications. The requirement to satisfy the statutory authorities is just one reason for documenting specifications of building siting, layout, intended use, means of escape in case of fire, appearance and many other factors. There are, of course, many detailed aspects of a building which can greatly affect its costs, including, for instance, the style of interior decoration, the quality of the fittings and installed equipment, and lighting and air-conditioning standards.

Disputes can be minimized, if not prevented altogether, when a contractor produces its own detailed project specification and asks the customer to accept it before the contract is signed. Any changes subsequently requested by the customer can then be identified easily as changes from the agreed specification and charged as additions to the original order.

Specifications for product development projects

Development programmes aimed at introducing additions or changes to a company's product range are prone to overspending on cost budgets and late completion. One possible cause of this phenomenon is that chronic engineer's disease which I call 'creeping improvement sickness'. Many will recognize the type of situation illustrated in the following example.

Case study

The project
A company producing electronic and audio equipment for domestic users has carried out a market survey. On the basis of this study the company plans to introduce a new 'fun' model stereo tape cassette player. The aim is a device with attractive styling, dual mains or battery operation, reasonable performance, but at a low price and calculated to appeal to the

tastes of teenage customers against the competition of foreign imports.

By any standards this can be regarded as a small project, requiring simple budgeting and a modest degree of programme control. It is certainly not dependent for its success on state-of-the-art project management techniques. Everything should be straightforward. Nothing can go wrong.

The kick-off meeting

The launch of the new product design can be visualized, starting with a meeting in the chief engineer's office in the company's development laboratories. In addition to the chief engineer the meeting would probably include representatives from other interested departments, such as sales and production. The other member needed to establish the necessary quorum is, of course, the design engineer (George) assigned to carry out the actual development work.

Discussion would undoubtedly focus on putting George on the right track to create the unit envisaged by the company's directors on the basis of the market survey. Thus George will be given a set of objectives. Let us assume, however, that, as often happens, these objectives are fairly broadly based and not written into a formal product specification.

George can be imagined emerging from the meeting, full of ideas arising from the discussion and carrying his own rough notes of the proceedings and perhaps a few sketches. He will undoubtedly have been given some idea of target production costs, styling, performance, the preferred selling price and an approximate date for stocks to be available for distribution and release to the market.

Initial design stage

We can safely assume that George will be fairly bubbling over with enthusiasm. Most competent engineers become keen when suddenly given responsibility for a new project on which their creative abilities can be unleashed. After a few weeks of activity behind the closed doors of his laboratory, George can be expected to emerge with the first experimental model of the new cassette player. This working model must then be subjected to the critical attention of various experts, among whom may be marketing staff, an industrial designer and production engineers or other suitable representatives of the department that will eventually have to manufacture the product.

Pre-production stage
Following successful evaluation of the prototype, and incorporation of recommendations from the experts, the next stage in the project will be the preparation of production drawings, bills of materials and specifications from which a small pilot production batch can be manufactured. One might reasonably expect, from experience, that this pre-production phase of the project would take considerably longer than the original design of the laboratory model. The production department may decide to go ahead with some limited tooling, and the production engineers and others will want to set up trial manufacturing procedures, check on tolerances, test-program any automatic operations and think generally about methods for assembly and testing.

Second thoughts
A period of waiting must be endured by George, during which, apart from having to check drawings or answer occasional production or purchasing queries, he is free to reflect upon his design. This leads him to have second thoughts. On thumbing through his component catalogues he has discovered that he could have specified a different amplifier, giving improved performance at a slightly reduced component cost.

Early modifications
George decides to implement the change which, incidentally, requires a redesign of the printed circuit boards at a stage when they have already been drawn and ordered in production prototype quantities. George puts the redesign in hand and cancels the order for prototype boards.

Modified drawings and parts lists are issued to the production and purchasing departments. The production cost estimators find that the cost saving expected from changing to the new amplifier will amount to less than 1 per cent of the total estimated production cost per unit. So far, the change has caused a three-week hold-up in the programme and preparatory work in several departments has had to be scrapped and restarted.

George, in the meantime, has received a visit from a representative of the company which he chose to supply the loudspeakers. The representative is delighted with the potential business but, taking a technical brochure from her briefcase, wishes George to know that she can offer, at modest cost, new loudspeakers that would suit the size and shape of the cabinet, extend the bass response by a whole octave, and be better able to withstand the increased power of the new amplifier. The slightly increased size of the replacement loudspeakers will result in further drawing modifications and the scrapping of some work already carried out on the pilot batch. George considers this a small price to pay for the significant increase in performance and decides to make the change.

Unforeseen problems
At length, and in spite of the delays and additional expense, the prototype batch is completed and passed back to the laboratory for evaluation. George is dismayed to find that every single one of the prototype batch exhibits two faults which were not apparent on the first laboratory-built experimental model. There is a significant amount of rumble from the tape cassette drive motor, now shown up as a result of the improvement in bass response. For the same reason, mains hum is audible.

Three possible choices are now open to George. He could revert to the original design, using the original amplifier and loudspeakers. George, however, has high ideals and the idea of degrading the performance does not appeal to him. The second option would be to introduce a simple filter circuit to cut the bass response to attenuate the rumble and hum. But this, again, would degrade the performance.

George decides that the third option is the only acceptable one. He modifies the mains power unit to remove the mains hum and specifies a higher quality tape drive motor to reduce the rumble. These changes, although they cause additional delay and costs, result in a prototype that finally passes all its tests.

It is time to evaluate the result.

A good result?
The eventual result is outstandingly good. The performance of the modified prototype measures up to George's most critical require-

ments. George is well pleased with the results of his labours and congratulates himself on a job well done.

The company's management is not so pleased. The oft-repeated phrase 'time is money' is as true in project management as anywhere, and it is usually fairly safe to assume that if the planned timescale has been exceeded, so have the budgeted costs. It is apparent that development costs have rocketed over budget in this case.

The manufacturing cost per unit has become so high that it will no longer be possible to sell the unit profitably at the intended price. In any case, the new model has been produced so late that the gap in the market where the demand originally lay has since been filled by a competitor's product.

All of this could have been prevented if George had carried out his original instructions. But what exactly were those original instructions? Where is the documentary proof? This simple example serves to show some of the pitfalls of a product development project that is not controlled from an adequate project specification.

George has, in fact, designed a very good product, but not the product which he was asked to design. He has allowed his own ideas to intrude and he has lost sight of the original objectives. George has fallen into a common trap by allowing the 'best' to become the enemy of the 'good'.

Case study revisited: how should it have been done?

It might be as well to take a second look at this imaginary project and see how the course of events would have run under a regime employing some of the fundamental elements of project control.

Written specification
The first noticeable difference would be the provision of a written project specification. The main part of this specification would be a technical product specification intended to clearly define all the design objectives from the start. Such product specifications should include an account of the expected performance, with quantified data, quality and reliability standards, styling guidelines, size and weight limits and so on.

Commercial objectives for the product development project

must also be specified. To assess the probable rate of return on capital investment (as part of initial project appraisal) the management must start with some idea of what this investment will be.

Budgets for development expenditure, production tooling and other costs should therefore be compiled and agreed at the beginning and recorded in the commercial part of the specification. The maximum permissible unit production cost and the target selling price must also be determined, both of these figures being related to sales forecasts giving the expected quantities to be produced for the first two or three years.

Finally, there is the question of timescale. The target date for market release has to be decided carefully. It must be an objective that can be achieved. Product release target dates are often chosen to allow the product launch announcement to be made at an important trade exhibition.

Planning and control

A more effective check could have been kept on progress in our example if a simple programme schedule (such as a bar chart) had been included as part of the project specification. Provided that this identified all the important project events ('milestones'), regular management checks would have revealed the danger of late running soon enough for corrective action to be taken.

Change control

Now suppose that George has reached the stage in the project where previously he was allowed to introduce his first design change (the amplifier). Under conditions of effective control he would not have been allowed to introduce any change after the issue of pre-production drawings and purchase requisitions without prior discussion with other departments likely to be affected.

It is usual for changes of this nature to be brought for approval before a representative 'change committee'. The committee will assess all the possible effects of any proposed change on stocks and work in progress, reliability, costs, timescale and so on before giving its consent or other instructions. We can be sure that at least some of the adverse effects of George's first change proposal would have been foreseen by a change committee. Apart from any technical reasons, this change would have been nipped in the bud because of the threat it posed to the timescale.

Procedures for controlling modifications are discussed in Chapter 11. It is enough at this stage to note that the other modifications which George introduced in the cassette player project would also have met with an early demise under a sound administration. George would have been kept on track by the formal product specification, by the sensible control of modifications and, of course, by the day-to-day supervision of his superiors.

Developing the project specification

Given the importance of specifying project requirements as accurately as possible, it is appropriate to end this chapter with some thoughts on the preparation of a project specification document.

Solution engineering

Although a customer might be clear from the very first about its needs, it is usual for dialogue to take place between the customer and one or more potential contractors before a contract is signed. During this process each competing company can be expected to make various proposals for executing the project that effectively add to or amend the customer's initial enquiry document.

In some companies this pre-project phase is aptly known as solution engineering. Each competitor arranges for its sales engineers to discuss the project details with the potential customer and work to recommend an engineering solution considered most likely to suit the customer's economic and technical needs. Solution engineering might last a few days, several months or even years. It can be an expensive undertaking (especially for the companies who fail to win the order).

It is tempting to imagine the chosen contractor's sales engineers settling down contentedly to write a single, definitive project specification, but the practice is likely to be quite different. The first draft descriptive text, written fairly early in the proceedings, will probably undergo various additions and amendments as the solution develops. It will probably be revised and re-issued more than once. The text will typically be associated with a pile of drawings, artists' impressions, flowsheets, schedules or other documents appropriate to the type of project. Those documents, too, might suffer several changes and re-issues before the agreed solution is reached.

A fundamental requirement when the contract is signed is to be able to identify positively which of these specification versions, which revision of the text and which issues of the other documents, record the actual contract commitment. Remember that the latest issue of any document might not be the correct issue.

The only safe way to identify any document is to label it with a unique serial or identifying number, and augment that by numbering each revision.

Format and content

The format described here is typical for a well-prepared project specification.

1 *Binder*   The specification for a large project is going to be around for some time and receive considerable handling. It deserves the protection of an adequate binder. The binder should be loose-leaf or otherwise allow the addition or substitution of amended pages.

2 *Specification identifier*   The binder should carry the specification serial (identification) number, the project number (if different) and the project title. All of these should be prominently displayed.

3 *Control schedule of specification documents*   This vital part of the specification complements the specification identifier by denoting the revision status of the complete document. Ideally it should be clipped in the folder along with the main text (either in the front or at the back). The control schedule must list every document which forms part of the complete specification. This includes drawings too large to be conveniently bound with the main text and other external documents that are relevant to adequate project definition (for example standard engineering specifications or statutory regulations).

   Minimum data required for each document are its serial and correct revision numbers. The title of each document should also be given. Should any of the associated documents itself be complex, it too should have its own inbuilt control schedule.

The control schedule should be given the same serial and amendment number as the document that it controls. If the specification is numbered XYZ123 and is at revision 6, then the control schedule itself should also be numbered XYZ123, revision 6. Thus the amendment state of the entire project specification (including all its attachments and associated documents) can always be identified accurately simply by giving one amendment number.

4 *Descriptive text* The narrative describing the project should be written clearly and concisely. The text should be preceded by a contents list and be divided logically into sections, with all pages numbered.

Every amendment must be given an identifying serial number or letter, and the amendment (or revision) number for the entire specification must be raised each time the text is changed. Amended paragraphs or additional pages should be highlighted, for example by placing the relevant amendment number alongside the change (possibly within an inverted triangle in the manner often used for engineering drawings).

5 *Supporting documents* Most project specifications need a number of supporting engineering and other documents that cannot conveniently be contained within the binder. These effectively form part of the specification and they must all be listed in the control schedule.

6 *Distribution list* A responsible person must keep a list of all those who received the initial issue of the specification. This can be used as a control document to make certain that all holders of the specification receive subsequent amendments. The safest form of control is to bind the distribution list in with all copies of the specification (although this can occasionally be politically undesirable).

Projects which are difficult or impossible to define

Most of the procedures and project cases described in this book are written from the project performer's (contractor's) point of view. They assume that the customer's project objectives and the contractor's commitments have been well defined in advance, enabling all stages of the project and its expenditure to be managed effectively against clear benchmarks.

Of course, there are times when a proposed project is so complex, or is fraught with so much uncertainty and risk, that its progress and outcome cannot be foretold at the beginning. In other words, it might simply be impossible for anyone to define the project accurately.

Using a feasibility study to improve early project definition

The investor faced with a very uncertain prognosis for a project might wish to start by commissioning a feasibility study from a consultant or professionally orientated contracting company to obtain more facts and expert advice. This approach is frequently used to examine and appraise the technical, logistical, environmental, commercial and financial aspects of all kinds of projects requiring major investment. Banks and other institutions asked to finance or otherwise sponsor ill-defined projects may require a satisfactory feasibility study report before committing funds. Government departments often demand or commission reports for projects which have national or international implications.

A feasibility study for a large capital project can be quite an undertaking in itself, perhaps taking years to prepare and costing millions of pounds. But a good feasibility study report can do much to point a project in the right direction and define its risks and achievable objectives.

A step-by-step approach to risk limitation

Another approach to starting an ill-defined project is to limit the risk by authorizing work step by step. It should be possible to divide the project into a number of stages for this purpose. Such stages might be set according to the following factors:

- The occurrence of significant events in the project that can easily be recognized when they occur or are achieved.
- The imposition of a time limit for each stage.

- A budgetary limit for each stage.
- A combination of any two or all of these.

Funding or authorization of expenditure on each new stage of the project would depend on a critical review of the results achieved and outlook for success as the previous stage nears its cut-off date. This approach has the advantage of limiting the committed risk and, whereas it is still not possible to define the whole project in advance, it should be possible to look the short way ahead necessary to define each limited step. Each step so defined may then be amenable to the project management procedures that cannot be used for the whole project.

Pure research projects are good examples of this phased approach. The initial setting up and provision of facilities can be regarded as the first stage and should be manageable as a definable project. Subsequent expenditure on the actual research, the results obtained and decisions about future funding can then be considered regularly at suitable intervals.

With the step-by-step approach it always has to be borne in mind that it might become necessary to abandon the project at any stage and write off the expenditure already incurred.

Some commercial safeguards

A contractor asked to embark upon a project in which its expected role is not adequately defined can, of course, accept the order, provided that the payment arrangements guarantee reimbursement of all the contractor's costs plus reasonable fees or profits. The contractor should ensure that the customer or investor bears the risk in these cases. Such arrangements can still be inconvenient or potentially difficult for contractors, because it might be difficult for them to arrange and commit resources for a project whose duration is unknown and which might have to be stopped at short notice.

It is common in construction projects to isolate any small parts of a project which cannot adequately be defined and which are outside the contractor's control, and list these separately in the quotation. An example would be a project to refurbish a building where part of the structure is hidden from view by wall cladding and is in uncertain condition. The proposal might assume the structure to be sound, but include a separate provisional estimate of costs that will be charged to the customer should additional work prove to be necessary when the cladding is eventually removed and the true state of the structure is revealed.

Risk analysis techniques

There are procedures which allow for probabilities or alternative options to be built into initial project planning, so that the project risks can be evaluated using statistical techniques. For an introduction to project risk analysis, see Simon, Hillson and Newland (1997).

Reference

Simon, P., Hillson, D. and Newman, K. (1997), *Project Risk Analysis and Management Guide*, Norwich, APM Group (for the Association for Project Management).

3

Organization

Every company has its own ideas about how to organize itself and its work. It is highly probable that if three companies doing similar work could be compared, three different organization structures would be found. Further, all three companies might be equally successful, implying that it is not always possible to say with determination or accuracy that there is one best organization solution.

This chapter cannot, therefore, declare exactly how every project should have its organization structured. Instead, it starts by setting out some of the properties that are required for efficient organization. It then describes possible organization options, together with their advantages and disadvantages.

For many project managers the following arguments will be academic, since they are often appointed within existing organizations and are given no authority or power to make significant changes. In those cases, this chapter is directed to the more senior management.

Effective organization and communications

An effective organization will have clear lines of authority and every member of the project will know what he or she must do to make the project a success. This is part of the management communication framework needed to motivate all the staff employed. A well-motivated group can be a joy to work with. A badly informed group, with vague responsibilities and ambiguous levels of status and authority, is likely to be poorly motivated, slow to achieve results, costly to run and extremely frustrating to work with.

The complement of good management communications is the provision of adequate feedback paths through and across the organization. These allow progress to be monitored, difficulties to be reported back to executive management and expert specialist advice on technical or commercial problems to be sought by any participant.

Project teams versus functional group or matrix organizations

Consider a company which is about to embark upon a project for the first time. A competent project manager is available, but this firm has never had to handle a complex capital project before and now has to set up the most suitable organization. If the project manager were asked to advise, he or she would immediately be faced with the question that often causes controversy:

- Should the company take all the key people destined to work on the project and place them under the direct management of the project manager, so that he or she is asked to manage a purpose-built project team?

Or, alternatively:

- Would it be better to have the project manager act in a purely functional capacity? He or she would still be responsible for the whole project, but with no direct authority over the workforce, having instead to coordinate the work provided from specialist groups and other departments, each of which is supervised by and reports directly to its own separate line manager within the company or wider organization.

Functional matrix organizations

Figure 3.1 shows an organization that is often called a functional matrix. Sometimes, for example, a manufacturing company occasionally has to handle a project that does not fit in with the routine production pattern. The company recognizes that there is no one in its normal line management structure who can logically oversee the special project. A project manager is, therefore, nominated to coordinate the work of all departments required to work on the special customer's project.

The power of the project manager in this kind of organization is usually very limited. The role is one of a facilitator or coordinator. The project manager has no line authority and cannot issue instructions to any departmental manager. Should any irreconcilable dispute arise, for example over work priority, the project manager must rely on the intervention of senior management to sort out the offending departmental managers.

Variations of the matrix organization

When a manufacturing company handles several projects simultaneously, it might appoint a project manager for each project and set up a matrix organization similar to that shown in Figure 3.2. A company engaged in petrochemical, mining or other large capital projects might operate a matrix organization along the lines of that shown in Figure 3.3.

The way in which power is apportioned between the project managers and the various departmental managers in a matrix can vary considerably from one company to another. The charts in Figures 3.2 and 3.3 cannot indicate where the most power lies and, therefore, remain valid for all the variations of the matrix that will now be described.

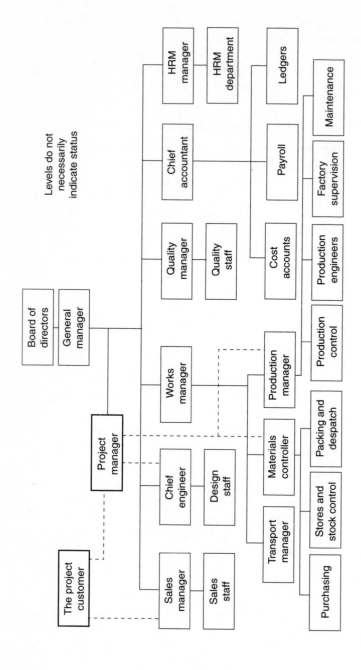

Figure 3.1 A functional matrix for a single project in a manufacturing company

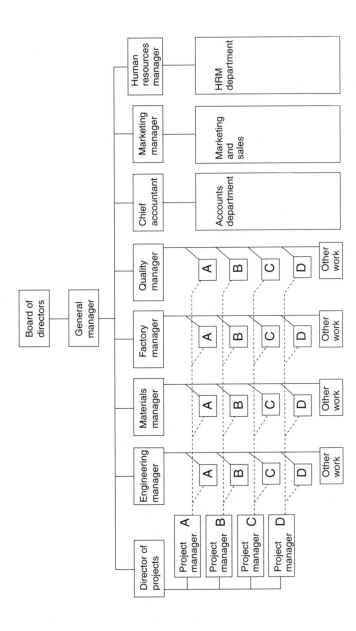

Figure 3.2 Matrix organization for several simultaneous projects in a manufacturing company

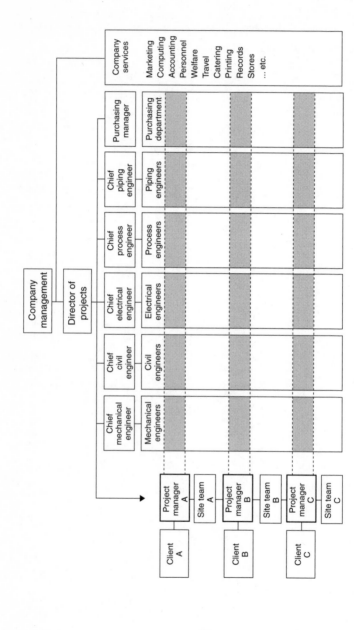

Figure 3.3 Matrix organization for a company engineering petrochemical, mining or large construction projects

Weak matrix

A weak matrix is similar to the functional matrix already described for the manufacturing company, except that it is generally used to describe an organization handling several projects at the same time. Each project manager is little more than a coordinator.

Balanced matrix

The balanced matrix (or overlay matrix) is very similar to a weak matrix and is sometimes described as such. In the balanced matrix, there is a declared balance of power and authority between the project managers and the functional department managers. They are expected to work together and agree the allocation of priorities and use of personnel and other resources to ensure the successful outcome of their projects.

This is perhaps the most common form of matrix. It is elegant in theory and enjoys many advantages over other forms of organization. It is not, however, as some have claimed, a universal solution for every project. All forms of the matrix have their advantages and disadvantages.

Project matrix

In a project matrix (or secondment matrix) the authority of the project managers is greatest and takes precedence over the authority of the functional managers, at least as far as work allocation and progressing is concerned. The intention here is that the functional managers nominate members of their departments to work for the project managers on their particular projects. The people assigned thenceforth report principally to the project managers (although they might remain physically located in their home departments).

Project team organization

It is, of course, possible to arrange things differently from the matrix options described above. A complete work group or team can be created for each project as a self-contained unit with the project manager placed at its head. The project manager is given direct line authority over the team.

The example shown in Figure 3.4 is a project team organization that might be set up for a petrochemical or mining project. This team should be able to carry out all the work necessary to devise the processes and reagent flows, specify and purchase the plant and equipment, and design the buildings and other facilities for a chemical processing plant. The project manager is in direct command, with complete authority for directing the participants so that the project meets all the objectives.

Communications across the various technical and professional disciplines are made easier when the project manager is in total command. All members of the team identify with the project and can (at least in the short term) be strongly motivated towards achieving the project goals. The key members of the team should preferably be located near each other, in the same building if possible.

Ideally, an office should be set aside for use as a 'project war room', where some or all of the team's managers can meet formally or informally whenever they wish, and where drawings, charts and plans can be displayed on tables and walls. War rooms for larger projects should also be equipped with appropriate means for communicating with computer and communication networks.

Project task forces in manufacturing

A complete, all embracing, self-contained project team can be impracticable to organize in a manufacturing company owing to the nature of the facilities and machinery required. Many of those facilities represent considerable capital investment and, together with their human operators, cannot be allocated full time to a single project, no matter how urgent the demands of that project might be. These facilities must be shared among all the projects and other work being undertaken by the company. Project managers cannot therefore be given direct line authority over any of those shared manufacturing functions and a matrix organization of some sort might be indicated rather than a pure team.

There are occasions, however, when the strong project focus and fast internal communications of a team are preferable to a

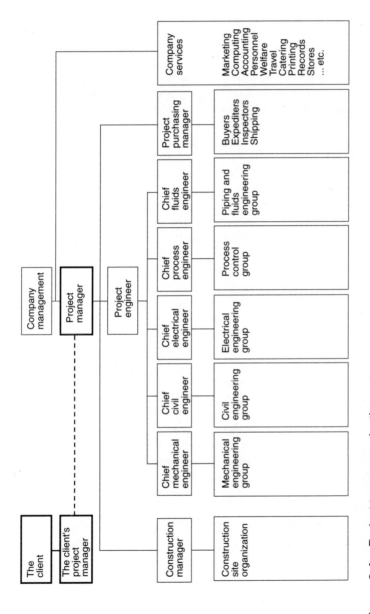

Figure 3.4 Project team organization

39

matrix. To take just one case, suppose that an important project is running extremely late and is in dire need of a rescue operation. In other words, there is an existing or impending crisis. In those circumstances, the company's management would be well advised to consider setting up a task force to finish the remainder of the project in the shortest possible time. But the problem remains of how to deal with manufacturing facilities that must continue to carry out other work.

A task force solution is possible. It depends on assembling managers (or their senior deputies) from all the departments involved in executing the project. A leader for this task force must be found, preferably from within the company. This person must possess determination and a positive outlook. He or she should also be experienced in the project management arts: if not, it might be prudent to engage an external consultant to provide urgent on-the-job training and guidance. The task force members will work more productively if they can be located together, away from their normal working locations. Better still, they should be provided with a dedicated office that can be used as their project war room. The result should be a powerful and effective management team with the expertise and authority to give the ailing project the best chance of recovery.

Although the project might still depend on the use of resources and facilities shared with other work, the seniority of the task force members should ensure that all critical project tasks get top priority. Suppose, for instance, that the machine shop is represented on the task force by its manager or a deputy. Then, when a critical project task requires the use of a machine that is used heavily for other work, the project leader is provided with a line of direct authority over the use of that machine through the senior machine shop delegate who is serving on the task force.

Which type of organization is best?

Team

Project teams have the advantage that they can each be directed to a single purpose: the successful completion of one project. A team can be completely autonomous. It is provided with and relies on its own resources. There is no clash of priorities resulting from a clamour of different projects in competition for common (shared) resources.

Much is rightly said and written about the importance of motivating people who work on projects. An important aspect of motivation is the generation of a team spirit, in which all members of the team strive to meet common goals. It is obviously easier to establish a team spirit when a project team actually exists, as opposed to the case where the people are dispersed over a matrix organization which has to deal with many projects.

If the work is being conducted for a government defence contract, or for any other project that requires a secret or confidential environment, the establishment of a project team greatly helps the organizers to contain all the work and its information within closed, secure boundaries.

Unless the project is very large, however, the individual specialist subgroups set up to perform all the varied activities within the project will prove too small to allow sufficient flexibility of labour and other resources. Where, for example, a common manufacturing facility of 100 people is coping with several projects, the absence of a few workers through sickness might result in some rescheduling but would be unlikely to cause disaster. If, on the other hand, a project team had been set up to include its own independent production group, perhaps needing only six people, the infection of three of these with flu could pose a more serious problem.

Inflexibility associated with small groups is seen more clearly in some of the experienced administrative and specialist discipline work functions, where it is often more difficult, if not impossible, to rectify matters at short notice using temporary employees. In the manufacturing case it is quite possible that only one or two people will be responsible for all project purchasing, or for project production control – indeed I have known one person to be made responsible for both of these activities on a small project team. In such circumstances, the fate of the project may depend on the capabilities and health of just one individual, who becomes virtually indispensable.

There is a danger that specialist engineers located in small project teams are deprived of the benefits of working in a department with colleagues of their own specialist discipline, namely the ability to discuss technical problems with their peers and having access to the valuable fund of general historic technical and professional data plus current awareness that such departments accumulate.

Even if a project is of sufficient size to justify its own exclusive team, not all the problems of project coordination will necessarily be overcome. Very often it might be found impossible to house all the participants under one roof, or even in the same locality. Although team organization might be logical and ideal for the project, a general lack of coordination between the functions is still a possible risk.

One problem with a project team organization is the question of what happens when the project comes to an end. When each project is finished and its team disbanded, the team members can suffer serious or even traumatic withdrawal symptoms. Organizational change usually brings problems, with dissatisfaction, rivalries and career worries created among those whose roles must change.

Another possible danger is that something could go seriously wrong with the project after its supposed completion, with expert attention required from the team's engineers to satisfy the customer and put matters right. If the team no longer exists, and the engineers who designed the project have been dispersed, events could take an embarrassing, even ugly, turn.

Matrix

The matrix option allows the establishment of specialist functional groups which have 'eternal life', independent of the duration of individual projects. This continuity of work promotes the gradual build-up of expertise and experience. Specialist skills are concentrated. Pooling of skills provides for flexibility in deploying resources.

Each member of every specialist group enjoys a reasonably stable basis for employment (provided the order book is full). There is a clear promotion path within the discipline up to at least chief engineer level, and each person in the group is able to compete against his or her colleagues for more senior positions within the group as vacancies arise in the long term.

Performance assessment of each individual, and any recommendation for promotion, improved salary or other benefits, is carried out by a chief engineer or other manager of the same engineering discipline within the stable group. This is more likely to result in a fair assessment and employee satisfaction. These possibilities are not readily available to the specialist engineer working alone in a multidisciplined project team.

The matrix organization has its own characteristic disadvantages. Not least of these is the split responsibility which each group member faces between the line manager and the project manager.

Summary

So, team or matrix? The arguments will no doubt continue as to which is the better of the two organizations. Some of the pros and cons are summarized in Figure 3.5. As a general rule (but it is dangerous to generalize in this subject) large projects of long duration will probably benefit from the formation of project teams. Matrix organizations are indicated for companies which handle a number of small projects in which neither the amount of resources nor the timescale needed for each project is great.

The hybrid option

Sometimes companies adopt the solution of a hybrid organization, operating a matrix organization in general, but with teams set up for certain projects when the need arises.

An example of such an organization is shown in Figure 3.6. It is arranged principally as a matrix, with specialist groups under their respective highly qualified and experienced chief engineers. The project management group contains project managers and project engineers who draw on the resources of the specialist groups for the skilled engineering and expert advice needed for most projects. If, however, a project should arise which is predominantly within one of the specialist skills, the company might decide to appoint a project manager from within the relevant specialist group, managing a team contained within the group.

Characteristic	Organization indicated	
	Team	Matrix
Maximum authority for the project manager	✓	
Freedom from duplicated or ambiguous lines of command	✓	
Maximum motivation of staff to meet difficult targets	✓	
High security of information: by enclosing work in secure areas	✓	
High security of information: by restricting the number of staff who need to know about the work	✓	
Most flexible deployment of resources		✓
Most effective use across the company of those with rare specialist skills or knowledge		✓
Large project, employing many people for a long duration	✓	
Several small simultaneous projects, each needing a few people for a short time		✓
Career motivation of individuals: opportunities for promotion within a person's specialist discipline		✓
Career motivation of individuals: through long-term continuity and relative stability of the organization		✓
Post-design support to construction or commissioning staff		✓
Efficient post-project services to the customer		✓
Establishment of 'retained engineering' information banks from which future projects can benefit		✓

Figure 3.5   Project team versus balanced matrix

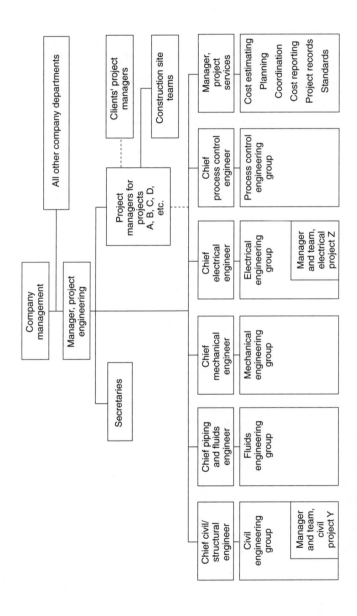

Figure 3.6 A hybrid organization

For example, a project to install a new electrical generator in an existing plant might be regarded as a project that could be handled entirely by a team within the electrical department. Similarly, a land reclamation project might be assigned solely to the civil engineering group, who would set up their own internal team to deal with it under a civil engineer as project manager.

Organizations with more than one project manager

In all probability the organization of any sizeable project will be found to contain more than one project manager.

When a company sells a project to a customer, that customer will probably wish to monitor progress in order to assure itself that there is every chance of the work being completed in accordance with the contract. For simple manufacturing contracts this role might be performed by the customer's purchasing department, using its expediting and inspecting personnel. But, except in this very simple case, the customer may wish to appoint its own project manager to oversee the contract. That is the situation in the example depicted in Figure 3.7. The customer will certainly need its own project manager where the project involves the customer in planning to accommodate, install and start up plant supplied under the project.

The project contractor is likely to be a major purchaser (that is, customer) having to buy expensive equipment or other items or services to be built into the project before it can be delivered to the end-user. For large projects some of these subcontracts could amount to significant projects in their own right, each needing planning and management similar to that used by the main contractor. Some subcontractors might need their own project managers to manage these subprojects. Indeed, the project contractor may even insist that such project managers are appointed, and might wish to inspect and approve the project management procedures used, possibly as a precondition of the subcontracts.

There is often more than one project contractor. Here is another reason for finding more than one project manager in the overall project organization. In such multi-contractor projects it is most probable that one contractor would be nominated by the project

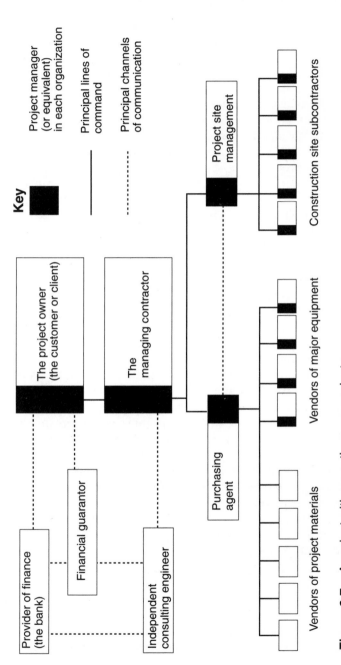

Figure 3.7 A project with more than one project manager
This is an example of a *contract matrix*.

Key

■ Project manager (or equivalent) in each organization

—— Principal lines of command

---- Principal channels of communication

Provider of finance (the bank)

Financial guarantor

Independent consulting engineer

The project owner (the customer or client)

The managing contractor

Purchasing agent

Project site management

Vendors of project materials

Vendors of major equipment

Construction site subcontractors

47

customer as the main or the managing contractor, with responsibility to the customer for managing or coordinating all the other contractors and subcontractors and completing the project.

Sometimes the customer will seek the services of an independent professional project manager, to act for the customer in return for a management fee. This role is often undertaken by companies, by professional partnerships or by professional people (such as consulting engineers or architects).

For very large projects several companies might agree to share the technical problems, expense (and risk) by forming a consortium or joint venture company, which adds yet another complication to the organization and at least one more project manager.

Whenever the complexity of a project is increased for any of these reasons, apart from the obvious need to define responsibilities carefully and tie up the contractual ends, it is vital that the lines of communication between all the parties are established and declared in a clear and efficient manner. It is not unusual to find projects where participants are separated by international borders and thousands of miles. The sheer volume of information, whether in the form of drawings, other technical documents, commercial correspondence, queries, and even hotel and travel arrangements, can be mind-boggling for a large project.

To avoid over-complicating what can already be an intricate organization, it makes much practical sense to nominate one individual in each of the organizations (including the customer) through whom all project information must be passed (in and out). Ideally, each organization will have its own project manager and they are the obvious nominees (even where, at some of the busier locations, the bulk of material actually requires a small army of clerks and other assistants to send/receive, sort, edit, distribute and file all the documents).

The project manager himself

Women in project management

Project manager *himself*? Before becoming too deeply involved with the subject of the project manager as a person, it is appropriate here to consider attitudes towards women in industry. In the UK, introduction of the Equal Pay Act (1970) and the 1975 Sex Discrimination Act is now history. Much is said and written about the need to give women fairer consideration for more senior management roles. Progress, however, is slow and industrial project management remains a male-dominated occupation. In the UK, for example, women account for only a very small proportion of the total membership of the Association for Project Management.

The good news is that the Association has a specific interest group, Women in Project Management, which is extremely lively and well supported by good attendance at its evening events and bi-annual conferences. The address of the Association for Project Management will be found on page 9.

Personality

What is the ideal personality for a project manager? If the objectives of project management could be condensed into responsibility for ensuring work completion within time and cost restrictions, then these goals could be achieved by a variety of approaches. One project manager might operate successfully by inducing fear and trepidation in his subordinates, so that his every word is seen as a command to be instantly obeyed. Another might achieve the same results through gentle but firm persuasion. The important element here is the ability to motivate people, by whatever means: the seasoned expert will be able to vary his or her management style according to the response of the individual being managed.

The average project participant will appreciate being led by a project manager who displays competence, makes clear decisions, gives precise, achievable instructions, delegates well, listens to and accepts sound advice, is enthusiastic and confident, and thus generally commands respect by example and qualities of leadership.

Perceptiveness and the use of project information

Other important characteristics of the project manager can be grouped under the heading of perceptiveness. Project managers must be able to select the salient facts from a set of data or a particular arrangement of circumstances. They must then be able to use these facts to best effect by taking action or reporting important exceptions to executive management, whilst filtering out the unimportant and irrelevant material.

Most project managers will become accustomed to being presented with information that is incomplete, unduly optimistic, inaccurate, deliberately misleading or completely wrong. Therefore it is important that project managers should not be gullible. They will learn to check much of the information which they receive, particularly by knowing what questions to ask in order to probe its validity. As they gain experience of a particular organization they should become capable of assessing the reliability of individuals or departments, so that they can apply 'confidence factors' to the data supplied by those individuals or departments and the stories that they tell.

The project manager as a hunter/gatherer of information

Project managers of any merit will know the frustration caused not simply through receiving inaccurate information, but also through receiving no information at all. Data deficiencies can take the form of delayed instructions or approvals from the customer, late information from subcontractors and vendors, and tardy release of design and other information within the project manager's own company. It can be difficult to obtain reliable and regular reports of cost and progress from far-flung project outposts, particularly where the individuals responsible feel themselves to be remote and outside the project manager's immediate authority or are educated to standards below those of the more developed nations.

The ability to gather and assess relevant data is, therefore, another requirement for project management. It is no good expecting to obtain the complete picture and manage a project simply by sitting behind a desk for the duration of the project. The project manager must take (and be seen to take) an active interest. He or she should visit personally and regularly those parts of the organization on which the project is dependent (a process sometimes known as 'management by walkabout'). It might be necessary for the project manager to visit vendors, subcontractors, the customer and a remote construction site at suitable intervals to gather facts, resolve local disputes, generate enthusiasm or simply to witness progress at first hand.

General knowledge and current awareness

Project managers in the age of technology could be described as specialists. Their background may be in one of the specialist engineering or other professional disciplines and they will certainly need to be trained in one or more of the current special project management techniques if they are to operate effectively. Nevertheless the term 'specialist' can be misleading, since much of the project manager's time will be taken up with coordinating the activities of project participants from a wide variety of administrative, professional, technical and craft backgrounds. This work, far from requiring specialization, demands a sufficient general understanding of the work carried out by those participants for the project manager to be able to discuss the work sensibly, understand all the commercial and technical data received and appreciate (or question) any reported problems.

The project manager should have a general understanding of administrative procedures as they will be applied throughout the project organization. If a person is asked to handle a flow of project data between different departments, he or she should be able to use their understanding of the administration and its procedures to arrange for the information to be presented in the form most likely to be helpful to the various recipients. In the jargon of computer technology, the project manager may be asked to solve interface problems, the solutions to which need some understanding of how the peripheral units operate.

There is little doubt that project management tools, techniques and philosophy will continue to undergo development and change. The project manager must be prepared to keep abreast of this development, undergoing training or retraining whenever necessary, and passing this training on to other members of the organization where appropriate. Some new developments will advance the practice of project management in general and others will not. Some practices and techniques will be more useful to a particular project than others and the project manager must be able to choose, use or adapt the most appropriate management methods for the particular project. The temptation to impose unsuitable methods on an organization for the sole reason that they represent the height of current fashion must be resisted.

Support, cooperation and training for the project manager

No matter how experienced, competent, enthusiastic and intelligent the person chosen for the job of project manager, he or she cannot expect to operate effectively alone, without adequate support and cooperation. This includes the willing cooperation of all staff engaged on the project, whether or not they report to the project manager in the line organization. It also includes support from higher management in the organization, who must at least ensure the provision of finance, accommodation, facilities, equipment, manpower and other resources when they are needed and the availability of suitable clerical or other supporting staff. Just as those working on the project need to be motivated, so too does the project manager, and supportive higher management who show constructive and helpful interest in the project can go a long way to achieve this. They can also help in the longer term by providing opportunities for training as new techniques or management systems are developed.

A person who is responsible for the allocation and progressing of project tasks will inevitably be called upon to decide priorities or criticize progress. The project manager must often arrange for the issue of work instructions in the full knowledge that he or she has no direct authority over all the departments involved. In a functional organization, departmental managers alone are responsible for the performance, day-to-day management and work allocation within their own departments. I have even known cases where departmental managers have told project managers to keep out of their departments. In such circumstances the project manager's influence can only be exerted as reflected authority from higher management, without whose full backing the project manager must be ineffective.

The main show of authority which the project manager can wield stems from his or her own personality and ability to persuade or motivate others. In these enlightened times discipline no longer implies the imposition of rigid authoritarian regimes nor management by fear through the constant threat of dismissal or other punitive action. Mutual cooperation and established job satisfaction are the more likely elements of an effective approach, especially in the long term. There will, however, be occasions when firm discipline has to be exercised; when, in the last resort, the full backing and support of higher management must be available as a reserve force which the project manager can call upon in any hour of need.

To maintain the company's competitive edge, the project manager should keep abreast of new developments in project control and management techniques and thinking. Senior management must recognize that much training is a continuous process and not simply a question of sending a person away for a one- or two-day course. Various training authorities arrange project management seminars where, in addition to the formal training given, delegates from different companies are able to meet and discuss common problems and solutions, and exchange views and experiences generally. The individuals involved and the profession as a whole must benefit from this type of exchange. It should also be remembered that the most effective learning is achieved from on-the-job training, which might need help from an external training consultant so that the training can be purpose-designed.

Just as important as the project manager's own training is the creation of an enlightened and informed attitude to modern project management methods among all those in the project organization. When the objectives of a particular project are outlined the project manager should ensure that participating managers, engineers and line supervisors have at least been given an elementary grounding in the appreciation of network analysis, scheduling, principles of cost and progress control, and the interpretation of associated computer reports. This should all be with specific relevance to the procedures chosen for use on the actual project. Training or instructions should be given in the use of the various forms and other documents that apply and (where appropriate) in the active use of relevant computer systems. There is a serious danger that people who are suddenly asked to work with unfamiliar techniques and procedures, without sufficient training or explanation, will fail to cooperate. People neglected in this respect cannot be expected to provide the necessary feedback and other responses. If participating staff understand the procedures and the reasons for them, their cooperation is far more likely to be forthcoming and effective.

Project services groups

Unless the organization is too small to support the additional expense, it makes sense to support the project management function by setting up a central project management services group. This is staffed with people (not too many!) who are capable of taking on the day-to-day chores of planning, resource scheduling, cost estimating, work progressing, cost and progress reporting and general supervision of the company's project management computer systems.

A project services group can be used in most kinds of project organizations. The group can be a functional department within a pure project team, where it will serve and report directly to the project manager. If the organization is a multiproject matrix or a hybrid organization, the services group can be established as one of the departmental functions (an arrangement illustrated in Figure 3.6).

A project services group concentrates a company's expertise in the techniques of project management just as any other functional grouping can enhance a particular professional discipline. Centralization helps to standardize project administration procedures across all projects in a company. A project services group can be the logical place in the organization from which to coordinate all parts of the project cycle, from authorization to closedown. It can administer procedures such as project registration and change control.

Some powerful project management computer systems, especially those handling multiproject scheduling, are best placed under the supervision of specially trained experts. Those experts must have a good working knowledge of all the organization's projects and combine that with special training in using the system and safeguarding the integrity of its database and back-up files. A central project services group is an excellent place in which to place that responsibility.

4

Work breakdown and coding

Any project has to be analysed and split into manageable tasks before it can be planned and implemented. However, some projects are so large that a more fundamental form of work breakdown must be undertaken, with the whole project broken up into a series of smaller projects, each of which might even have its own project manager and sub-organization. This chapter first considers the breakdown of such large projects, and then goes on to discuss the way in which all projects, regardless of their size, need to be divided into sensibly coded elements or work packages.

Family tree hierarchy

Work breakdowns must be carried out in a systematic fashion, so that there is a logical, hierarchical pattern to the breakdown (in the fashion of a family tree). The importance of this structural relationship between different constituents of the work breakdown has led to widespread acceptance and use of the term 'work breakdown structure', which is commonly abbreviated to WBS.

Logical interfacing and completeness

In addition to regarding the work breakdown as a family tree, it is also possible to visualize it as a jigsaw puzzle, with every piece put in its right place and with no piece missing. This concept is useful on two counts:

1   A method must be found that clearly and simply identifies each piece of the puzzle and its place in relation to all the other pieces. This objective can be achieved by giving each piece an identification number which, through the use of a carefully devised, logical system, acts as a locator or address (discussed in the following section of this chapter).

2   When the work breakdown is produced every piece of the puzzle must be included, with no piece missing to spoil the total picture. This objective is more difficult, but the risks of omission can be reduced by the use of suitable checklists.

Work breakdown structures for large projects

Consider a project to develop a mining complex or other plant for on-the-spot extraction and processing of mineral resources in an area that was previously uninhabited and which is many miles from the nearest railhead, port or airport. The project for building the plant would cost hundreds of millions of pounds, but that would represent only one aspect of the total work. It might be necessary to build roads, possibly a railway, an airstrip, housing, schools, churches, hospital, shops and indeed a whole township (all of which would constitute the project infrastructure).

Now imagine trying to estimate the cost of such a large project, and attempting to establish budgets and plans against which to manage the work. Many projects, even if they are not on this grand scale, are too complex to be estimated, planned and controlled effectively unless they are first divided into smaller subprojects. Each of these subprojects must then itself be further divided into smaller work packages and tasks.

The work breakdown structure for a large mining project is shown in Figure 4.1. This illustration shows the large work packages identified at the start of the breakdown. In practice the process of work breakdown would continue, leading to more and smaller packages until, right at the bottom, the individual tasks and purchases are reached.

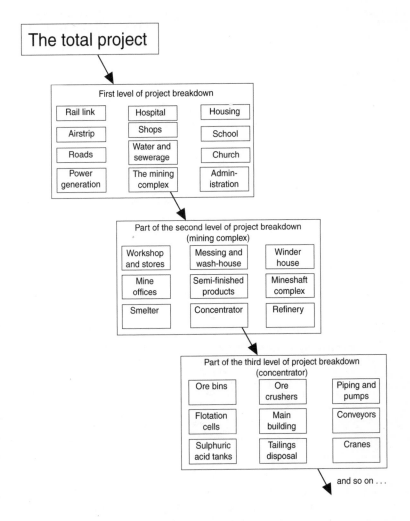

Figure 4.1   Part of the work breakdown for a large mining project

Coding systems

Those responsible for designing any coding system, whether it is for costs or for document numbers, must always bear in mind that it should not be treated in isolation from other management and engineering information systems in the company. There are many advantages if the same system can be applied over all a company's projects, and across other areas of the company's activities.

Functions of code

A code is a shorthand method for conveying information about an item. For project management purposes an item might be anything from the whole project to a small part of it, physical or abstract. It could be a component, a drawing, a job, a manufacturing operation, a piece of construction work, an engineering design activity – anything, in fact, which is necessary for the project. What all these items have in common is that they are almost always associated with cost. Every item (either by itself or grouped with others) has costs that must be estimated, budgeted, funded, spent, measured, reported, assessed and (where appropriate) recovered.

There are many reasons for allocating codes to items, rather than simply describing them in words. For example, properly designed codes can be precise and unambiguous. They also have the advantage, essential in computer systems, of facilitating filing, analysis, editing and sorting for reporting and control.

The functions of a code include the first or both of the following:

1   A code must act as a unique name that *identifies* the item to which it refers.
2   The identifying code, either by itself or by the addition of subcodes, can be arranged so that it categorizes, qualifies or in some other way *describes* the item to which it relates.

The best coding systems are those which manage to combine both these functions as simply as possible in numbers that can be used throughout a company's management information systems.

Typical examples

Three different examples are presented here to demonstrate the use of codes. Figure 4.2 is an imaginary example based on a radio engineering project. Figures 4.4 and 4.5, for heavy engineering and mining projects, are based on actual company cases. Although all of these examples are from engineering projects, the general principles apply to all projects.

Radio engineering project
Consider a project to design and build equipment for a radio-communication link. Figure 4.2. shows the coded work breakdown, set out in hierarchical (family tree) fashion. The chart shows only the higher levels of the work breakdown. Space does not allow listing of the hundreds of codes that would be allocated to the many components at all the lower levels, but we can include a few examples from each level. Information about these is shown in the box at the right-hand side of Figure 4.2.

At the top level, the project has been given the number 110-0000. This identifies the project for all accounting, engineering and manufacturing purposes.

Each number, provided it is unique within the system, is an unambiguous way of naming any item. In practice, however, it is always wise to bracket a concise verbal description with the number whenever the item is referred to, as a simple precaution against clerical errors. Thus it is always better to refer to an item as 'Transformer 110-2210' in documents rather than just 'Item number 110-2210'.

Further examination of Figure 4.2 shows that the code numbers have been designed to correspond with the work breakdown structure or family tree. The fact that Transformer 110-2210 has a cost and part number starting with the string 110-22 identifies the transformer as being used on Modulator 110-2200 which, in turn, is used on Project 110-0000. This numbering process is continued throughout the work breakdown, so that even individual components can be given codes that relate to the hierarchy. This is illustrated in Figure 4.3, where the code number for the bobbin used on Transformer 110-2210 is analysed.

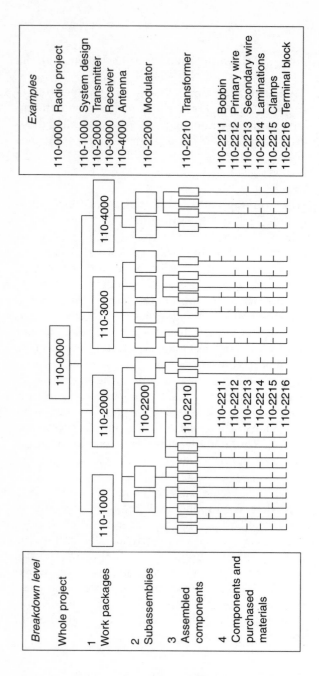

Figure 4.2 Work breakdown and cost coding for a radiocommunication project

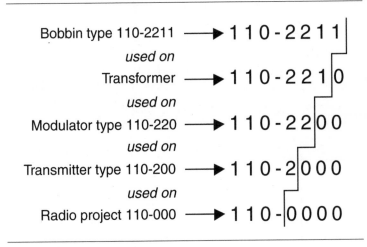

Figure 4.3 A low-level work breakdown and cost coding example for the radiocommunication project

The task for winding and assembling the purpose-built transformer 110-2210 might be given a related cost code, such as 110-2210C, where the 'C' suffix denotes the coil winding operation. A two-digit suffix is more often used instead of a single letter, allowing greater scope for detailed breakdown.

A one- or two-digit subcode is often added to show which department is responsible for a particular task or cost item. Yet more digits can be added to denote the trade or engineering discipline involved.

Consider, for instance, the activity of designing Transformer 110-2210. The cost code might be 110-2210-153, with the three-digit subcode 153 in this case showing that the engineering department (1) is responsible for the task, the engineering discipline is electrical (coded [5]), and the last digit (3) indicates the grade of person (for example senior engineer, engineer or designer) normally expected to carry out the task of designing this transformer. Because this final digit is directly linked to a grade of labour it might also denote a standard cost rate per hour.

Two more project examples

It is possible to design the project numbering method in a way that allows each number to signify certain key information about its project, in addition to acting as a simple identifier. Numbers can also be made to convey descriptive information about items. Examples of these applications are given in Figures 4.4 and 4.5.

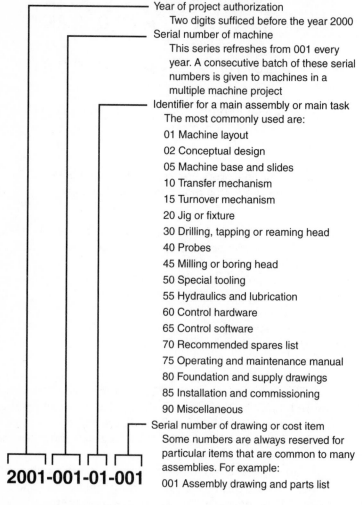

Year of project authorization
   Two digits sufficed before the year 2000
Serial number of machine
   This series refreshes from 001 every
   year. A consecutive batch of these serial
   numbers is given to machines in a
   multiple machine project
Identifier for a main assembly or main task
   The most commonly used are:
   01 Machine layout
   02 Conceptual design
   05 Machine base and slides
   10 Transfer mechanism
   15 Turnover mechanism
   20 Jig or fixture
   30 Drilling, tapping or reaming head
   40 Probes
   45 Milling or boring head
   50 Special tooling
   55 Hydraulics and lubrication
   60 Control hardware
   65 Control software
   70 Recommended spares list
   75 Operating and maintenance manual
   80 Foundation and supply drawings
   85 Installation and commissioning
   90 Miscellaneous
Serial number of drawing or cost item
   Some numbers are always reserved for
   particular items that are common to many
   assemblies. For example:
   001 Assembly drawing and parts list

2001-001-01-001

Figure 4.4   System of codes used by a heavy engineering
company

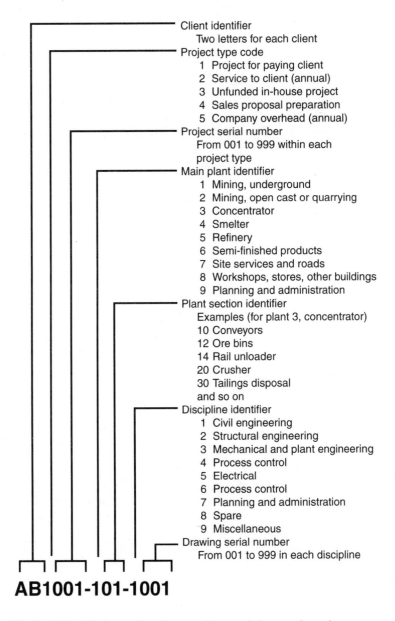

Client identifier
   Two letters for each client
Project type code
   1 Project for paying client
   2 Service to client (annual)
   3 Unfunded in-house project
   4 Sales proposal preparation
   5 Company overhead (annual)
Project serial number
   From 001 to 999 within each
   project type
Main plant identifier
   1 Mining, underground
   2 Mining, open cast or quarrying
   3 Concentrator
   4 Smelter
   5 Refinery
   6 Semi-finished products
   7 Site services and roads
   8 Workshops, stores, other buildings
   9 Planning and administration
Plant section identifier
   Examples (for plant 3, concentrator)
   10 Conveyors
   12 Ore bins
   14 Rail unloader
   20 Crusher
   30 Tailings disposal
   and so on
Discipline identifier
   1 Civil engineering
   2 Structural engineering
   3 Mechanical and plant engineering
   4 Process control
   5 Electrical
   6 Process control
   7 Planning and administration
   8 Spare
   9 Miscellaneous
Drawing serial number
   From 001 to 999 in each discipline

AB1001-101-1001

Figure 4.5   System of codes used by a mining engineering company

The convenience of grouping items into families of items with common or similar characteristics is important for many comparative purposes. Family grouping and identification can be built into item codes using suitable digits as subcodes. A family might comprise, for example, all pumps specified by a mining or petrochemical company. Another example might be that the subcode digits 01 appearing in a particular place in the item code for a piece of manufactured equipment would always indicate the mainframe assembly. The systems shown in Figures 4.4 and 4.5 both include such family identifiers.

Another type of family is encountered when considering machined objects that share manufacturing similarities by virtue of their shape and the machining operations to be performed; an application of family coding which is vital to the manufacture of components in group technology cells.

Benefits of a logical coding system

Although the primary purpose of a coding system might be to identify parts or to allocate costs, there are many benefits available to the company which is able to maintain a logical coding system in which all the codes and subcodes have common significance throughout the company's management information systems. These benefits increase with time and the accrual of records, provided that the system is used consistently without unauthorized adaptations or additions. The benefits depend on being able to retrieve and process the data effectively.

If a coding system is designed logically, taking account of hierarchical structure and families, and is well managed, some or all of the following benefits can be expected:

● Easy retrieval of items from records of past projects which correspond to or are similar to items expected in new projects. This is essential as a basis for making comparative cost estimates.

● Easy retrieval of design information (especially flowsheets, calculations and drawings) for processes, assemblies or components used on past projects which are similar to those needed for a new or current project. This 'retained engineering' can result in a considerable saving of engineering design work, time and costs if all or part of the previous design can be reused or adapted. Not only does such design retrieval avoid the unnecessary costs of designing everything afresh, but it also allows the new project to incorporate designs that have already been proven or debugged, so that the scope for errors is reduced.

● Rapid identification of purchase requisitions and specifications from previous projects for equipment which corresponds to new requirements. This is another example of retained engineering which can speed the preparation of new purchase specifications (especially when the main texts of the former specifications can be retrieved from files in a word processor).

● Grouping of components into families according to their basic shapes and sizes, relevant to the manufacturing processes needed, to maximize production engineering efficiency (as in the case of group technology cells).

● If it is possible to use a common system, cost estimates, budgets, recorded costs, drawing schedules and many other documents and tasks on the project plan can all be related in a database for project administration, management reports and control.

● The ability to carry out statistical analysis on cost and other records from past projects for a variety of reasons, including monitoring performance trends. The following examples from my own experience were extremely useful in a heavy engineering company and illustrate only two of the many possibilities for exploiting properly coded records:

1 The averaging of recorded costs for commonly recurring tasks from many past projects allowed the preparation of project estimating tables (expressed in man-hours and updated materials costs). These tables proved very useful for scheduling new projects and for making global checks on detailed cost estimates for new project proposals.

2   Analysis of detailed and accurately coded past shipping records enabled a table to be compiled showing average and probable maximum shipping weights for categorized items used on different types of heavy engineering projects. With the help of a shipping company the table was developed for presentation to the materials control manager as a 'ready-reckoner', which, with occasional updating, was greatly appreciated and used effectively for estimating project shipping weights and costs to all relevant countries.

Choosing a coding system

Once a coding system has been established it is difficult and unwise to make any fundamental change. The choice of a system therefore has to be undertaken with a great deal of care. It should be regarded as a long-term investment. Suppose that a company has been operating for many years with a comprehensive coding method, applied right across all its systems for drawing and other document numbering, cost estimating, cost accounting and part numbering. If this company makes a change to the numbering system, so that numbers which previously had one meaning now denote something entirely different, some of the following problems can arise:

1   Drawings filed under two different systems.
2   Similar inconvenience caused to long-standing customers who maintain their own drawing files for projects.
3   No easy way of identifying similar previous jobs for the purpose of comparative cost estimating.
4   Difficulty in retrieving earlier designs.
5   Staff have to learn and live with two or more systems instead of one.
6   Problems for storekeepers, with two different systems for part numbers. Parts common to earlier projects may have to be renumbered for newer projects, so there is a possibility of identical common parts being stored in two places with different part numbers.

7 Mayhem created in any attempt to use a relational database that relies on code numbering.

The need for simplicity

This is the place to insert a word of warning. It is possible to be too ambitious and try to make numbers include too much information. The result can be numbers that are 14, 15 or even more digits long. The designer of such a system may feel very proud, and computer systems are well able to accept and process such numbers. But please remember the human element – the 'people interface'. People are going to have to work with these numbers, entering them in written or electronic records. In some cases numbers have to be used on project sites, in high winds, driving rain or other hostile conditions. Think of the user. Simple codes use less clerical time and result in fewer errors.

What happens when the customer says 'Use my coding system!'?

Not infrequently, an irritating problem arises when customers insist that their own numbering system is used, rather than that normally operated by the project contractor. This happens particularly when a customer is to be presented with a complete set of drawings as part of the contract and wants to be able to file these along with all the other drawings in its own system. This, unfortunately, is a case where 'the customer is always right'.

This problem of having to use customers' numbering systems is usually restricted to drawings but in some projects it can apply to equipment numbers or part numbers. It also occurs, and is a great nuisance, in the cost coding of work packages or purchased plant for major projects, where the customer and contractor must work together to request, authorize and arrange the release of funds (either from the customer's own resources or from another financing organization). In such cases the customer might insist that all estimates, budgets and subsequent cost reports for the project are broken down against its own capital appropriation or other cost codes.

Three options
There are three options to consider when the customer asks the contractor to use a 'foreign' coding system.

1   Say 'No!' to the customer. The person who adopts this course is either courageous or foolhardy. It might even be impossible to do so under the terms of contract. In any case, it would be a short cut to achieving bad customer relations or losing the customer altogether.

2   Change over completely to the customer's system for the project in question. In this case the contractor calls the project a 'special case', abandons the in-house system, asks the customer for a set of its procedures and uses those for the project. This option cannot be recommended for the following reasons:

- The information management benefits of the in-house system would be lost for all data for the project.
- It will soon be discovered that every project is a 'special case'. The contractor might soon have to operate as many different coding systems as there are customers.

3   Use both systems simultaneously. This option, the sensible compromise course, offers the only acceptable solution. Every drawing and other affected item must be numbered twice, once for each system. Everything must, of course, be diligently cross-referenced between the two systems. This is tedious, time-consuming and means that staff have to learn more than one system. At one time it would have caused sufficient extra work to provide a weak argument for trying to obtain extra reimbursement from the customer. Fortunately, computer systems can greatly reduce the effort needed for cross-referencing, sorting and retrieving data numbered under duplicate systems.

5

Cost estimating

An accurate estimate of project costs is necessary for subsequent management decisions and control. The most obvious reason for producing cost estimates is to assist in pricing decisions, but estimates are usually needed for all commercial projects, including in-house projects and those sold without fixed prices. Timescale planning, pre-allocation of project resources, the establishment of budgets for funding, manpower and cost control, and the measurement of achievement against expected performance all demand sound estimates.

Cost format

The estimator should have a working knowledge of the way in which the organization's cost accounting system operates. Figure 5.1 shows a typical distribution of the costs for an industrial project.

The bottom item shows direct labour costs, which are all the man-hours that can be directly attributed to the project multiplied by their appropriate cost rates. In some companies, a labour

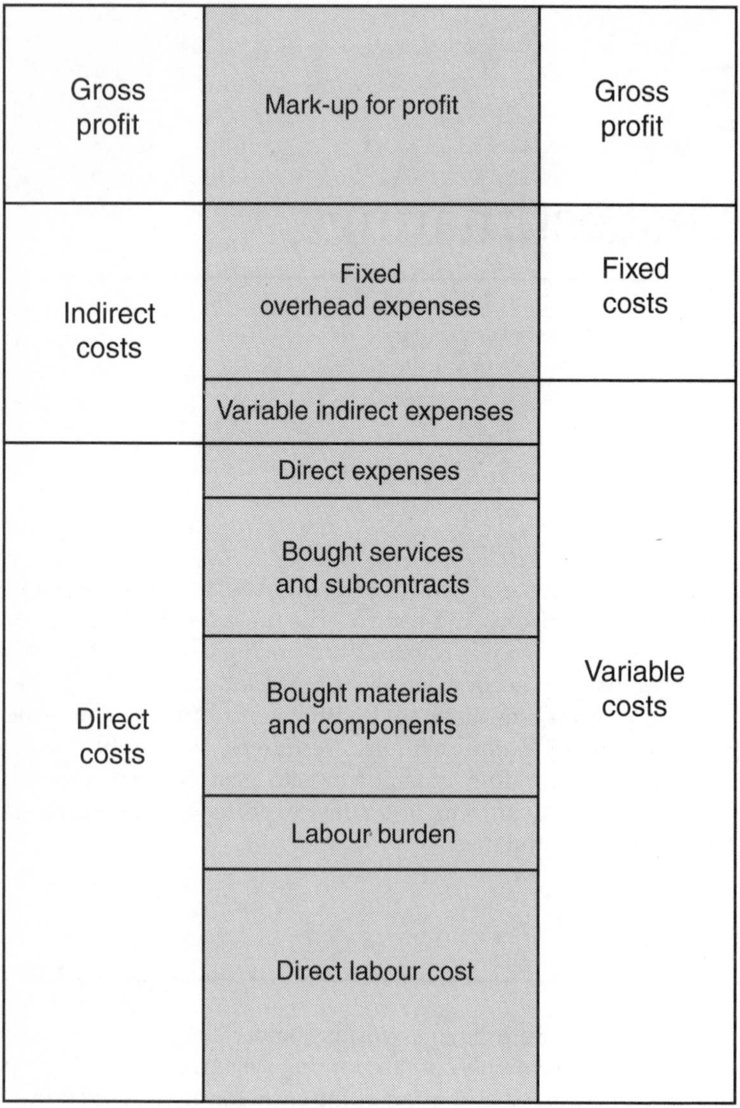

Gross profit	Mark-up for profit	Gross profit
Indirect costs	Fixed overhead expenses	Fixed costs
	Variable indirect expenses	Variable costs
Direct costs	Direct expenses	
	Bought services and subcontracts	
	Bought materials and components	
	Labour burden	
	Direct labour cost	

Figure 5.1 A typical cost structure

burden is added, pro rata, to these costs to cover such items as National Insurance contributions and non-salary benefits.

Other costs in the illustration are classed as either direct or indirect, the distinction again being whether or not these costs can be directly attributed to the project. The rate at which direct costs are incurred varies with the rate of working on the project, and most direct costs are therefore classed not only as direct costs but also as variable costs.

Indirect costs include all general expenses of the organization, such as management and general administration, accommodation, heat, light, business rates and so on. These costs tend to be incurred at a constant rate, whether the project is active or not, and most indirect costs are therefore also known as fixed costs.

Indirect costs do not usually have to be estimated in detail by the project estimator, because they can be added pro rata to the direct labour costs at a rate based on calculations made by the company accountant.

Although fixed costs can differ slightly from overhead costs (as shown in Figure 5. 1), for practical purposes fixed costs are usually approximately the same as overheads, and variable costs are almost equivalent to direct costs.

Estimating accuracy

It is clear that the better the project is defined at the outset, the less chance there should be of making estimating errors. However, the possibility of error can never be eliminated, and no sensible person could ever declare project cost estimates to be accurate. Estimating always involves an element of personal judgement. Most projects will produce surprises, usually unwelcome. If the final project costs do happen to coincide with the estimates, that might be a cause for celebration but it would usually be pure chance.

The cost estimator's task is to use all the data and time available to produce the best estimate possible. That is, a carefully calculated judgement of what the project *should* cost if all goes according to expectations. Estimates made with a high degree of confidence will greatly assist those responsible for any competitive pricing decision, and accurate estimates improve the effectiveness of cost budgets and resource schedules.

Classification of estimates according to confidence

Some companies classify cost estimates according to the degree of confidence that the estimators can express in their accuracy. These classifications depend on the quality of information available to the estimators and the time allowed for preparing the estimates. Different organizations have their own ideas on this subject, but here are three categories that are in common use.

1   *Ballpark estimates* are those made when only rough outline information exists. Ballpark estimates are also made in emergencies, when there is no time to prepare a detailed estimate. A ballpark estimate might achieve an accuracy of ±25 per cent, given a very generous amount of luck and good judgement, but far wider divergence is to be expected.

2   *Comparative estimates* are made by comparing work to be done on a new project with similar work done in the past. They can be attempted before detailed design work takes place, without accurate materials lists or work schedules, but an outline project specification is essential. It might be possible to achieve ±15 per cent accuracy. Comparative estimates are commonly used as the basis for tenders.

3   *Feasibility estimates* can be derived only after a significant amount of preliminary project design has been carried out. In construction projects, for example, the building specification, site data, provisional layouts and drawings for services are all necessary. Quotations must be obtained from the potential suppliers of expensive project equipment or subcontracts, and material take-offs or other schedules should be available to assist with estimating the costs of materials. The accuracy for feasibility estimates should be better than ±10 per cent. This class of estimate is often used for construction tenders.

The degrees of accuracy quoted in these examples are about as good as could ever be expected. Many organizations will assign wider limits. It is also common to find asymmetric limits, slewed about zero. A company might, for example, work on the assumption that its ballpark estimates are accurate to within +50 or −10 per cent.

Standard tables

In some industries, particularly construction and civil engineering, there are standard texts and tables available to help the estimator. Companies operating in those industries will undoubtedly employ professional staff who know how to estimate quantities and working rates and convert these to costs from their standard tables. This chapter is directed more at those who do not have access to such data and in-house expertise.

Profit vulnerability

The vulnerability of planned profits to costs which exceed estimates is not always appreciated. Suppose that a project was sold for a fixed price of £1m against a total cost estimate of £900 000. The budgeted gross profit was therefore £100 000, or 10 per cent of the selling price.

Now suppose that the project actually cost £950 000. The difference between the actual cost and the estimated cost (the estimating error) was only about 5.6 per cent. But gross profit has been slashed from the expected £100 000 to only £50 000, an error of not 5.6, but 50 per cent.

Planned profits are always subject to many risks. Some of these can be predicted but others can not. The aim is to identify and allow for quantifiable risks as far as possible, and then to provide a sensible contingency allowance to offset the unpleasant surprises.

Compiling the task list

The first stage in cost estimating is to list all known items that are going to attract expenditure. This may prove difficult. But any item inadvertently left out of the cost estimates will result in an underestimate for the project as a whole.

Preparation of a work breakdown (as a family tree or 'goes into' chart), complete with cost codes, is a logical way of considering the total project and should reduce the risk of errors of omission. But at the outset of a project the work breakdown usually has to be compiled in fairly broad terms, because much of the detail will remain unknown until the project has advanced well into its engineering design phase (long after the contract has been signed and everything has become a firm commitment).

Using checklists

One very useful way of helping to prevent forgotten tasks is to use checklists. Every company with sufficient experience can develop these (see Figure 2.2 for instance). A full checklist would include all possible factors – technical, commercial, statutory, environmental, social and so on – that might eventually have a bearing on the work and its costs.

Checklists can prove to be long and detailed documents. Typically they list as many possibilities as the compiler can think up, so they inevitably include some irrelevancies and can seem tedious. It is, however, in this very wealth of detail that the importance and strength of checklists lie.

Software tasks

The task list must include not only all the obvious items of project hardware, but also every associated software job. 'Software' is a very familiar term in the context of computers and IT projects, but projects quite remote from computer work have their own software. Schedules for production inspection and testing, instruction and maintenance manuals, lists of recommended spares and consumables may have to be specially written. These, together with any other documentation specified in the proposal or contract, are software tasks which must usually be allowed for in the estimated costs.

Forgotten tasks

Activities often forgotten during the estimating phase of manufacturing projects, only to be remembered too late for inclusion in the project budgets (and price), include incidental production processes such as paint spraying, inspection and testing. In some firms these may be covered by the general overhead rate, but in many others they will not and must be listed among the direct cost estimates. Protective plating, silk screen printing, engraving and so on are frequently omitted from estimates. For construction projects there can be many easily forgotten site expenses, such as the provision of site huts and other facilities.

An expensive item, sometimes neglected during project cost estimating, is the work entailed in final commissioning, handover and customer acceptance of the completed project. Contracts often demand that the contractor provides training facilities for some of the customer's operatives or technicians. Training sessions can involve the contractor's senior engineers in much hard work, both in the actual training and in preparing the training material beforehand.

Documentation

Completion of a work breakdown structure or, failing that, a simple task list has established a basis on which project estimates can be made. When the estimates are collected for any project of significant size, a large amount of data will be assembled. These data should be presented in a tabular arrangement to allow easy reference, detailed analysis and extension into total amounts – for departments and for groups of tasks.

A certain amount of procedural discipline has to be imposed on the estimating function throughout the organization, and from one project to another. Estimates should be set out according to a standard company procedure, itemized where possible by cost codes within the work breakdown structure. This will facilitate comparison between the estimates and the cost accountant's records of the actual costs eventually incurred, on a strict item for item basis. This is essential as part of the cost control function. As experience and data build up over a few years, it will also contribute to the accuracy of comparative estimates for new projects.

Standard format

Estimates should be set down in a standard and logical manner. Calculations performed in odd corners of notebooks, on scraps of paper and on the backs (or fronts) of envelopes are prone to error and premature loss. They will be unlikely to fulfil any of the conditions already mentioned. In other words, standardized estimating forms are needed (either as hard copy or as forms on a computer screen).

Project estimating forms can be arranged to fit in with the kinds of work breakdown structures that were shown in Figures 4.2, 4.4 and 4.5. One sheet can be allocated to each main project work package or group of tasks, while every row on the forms would be occupied by one task or activity. Adding the costs along each row yields the estimated cost of the relevant task (which can, incidentally, be very convenient for pricing spare parts). Totalling relevant columns gives the commitment expected for each department, and the results can be used to help with departmental budgeting and coarse resource scheduling.

Attempts to design estimating forms will fail if they are over-ambitious. There is no need to provide a column for every contingency. Instead, one or more columns can be left with their headings blank, to be filled in as required for any special purposes.

An example of a general purpose estimating form is given in Figure 5.2. This allows six different grades of labour to be shown and assumes that all hours will be costed at the appropriate standard cost rates. It is likely that a company might need more than six different standard cost grades throughout a project cost estimate, but it is far less likely that more than six grades will be needed for all the jobs listed on one sheet. The cost estimator will therefore be able to allocate the labour columns (numbered 4 to 9 on this example) to the range of grades necessary for the work being estimated on each particular sheet.

The standard grade code and rate should be entered in the

COST ESTIMATE

Estimate for:

| | | Project number or sales reference: | | | | | | | | | | Estimate number: Case: Date: | | |
| | | | | | | | | | | | | Compiled by: | | Page of |

1	2	3	4	5	6	7	8	9	10	11	12	13	14	15
			Labour times and costs by department or standard grade						Total direct labour cost	Overhead cost %	Materials			Total cost 10+11+ 12+13
Code	Item	Qty									Standard or net cost	Burden %	Longest delivery (weeks)	
			Hrs	£	Hrs	£	Hrs	£	Hrs	£	Hrs	£	Hrs	£					

Figure 5.2 General purpose cost estimating form for manufacturing projects

77

space at the head of each column to show the rates that were current at the time of estimating.

There is no need to complicate a general purpose estimating form by adding extra columns for such things as special tooling. Such items can easily be accommodated by designating them as separate tasks in their own right. Each can be entered on a row, and the costs added up along the row in the same way as any other task.

The inclusion on the general purpose form of a column headed 'longest delivery' in the materials section is not connected directly with cost estimating. However, the people who enter the material costs on the form are also the people who can provide information on expected delivery times, and it is better and more efficient to gather all these data from them as early as possible and at the same time. By including longest lead time estimates, the usefulness of these forms is immediately extended, enabling them to be used as a valuable source of information for subsequent timescale planning.

Collecting departmental estimates

Estimating is often regarded as an unpleasant task, a chore to be avoided at all costs if other priorities can be found as an excuse. Therefore a more direct approach is needed to all those who are expected to provide cost estimates for a project.

In recent years networked computers have presented another method for gathering information from a number of different sources and, no doubt, some companies can adapt this method for compiling project estimates. In fact, some project management software, although designed originally for planning and control, allows system users to enter estimating data to the project database. However, this still relies on the goodwill of people.

Short of applying legal compulsion or threat of physical violence, personal canvassing is the best way to get quick and dependable results. The process starts by preparing a complete set of estimating sheets for the project, with every known task listed and cost-coded. The sheets should be arranged in logical subsets according to the work breakdown structure. The project manager or delegate can then embark on a tour of all the departments involved, installing him- or herself purposefully at each manager's desk in turn. The aim is to remain firmly rooted in each department until all the desired data have been extracted. The person performing this task may become unpopular in the process, but being well-liked is not the most important aspect of a project manager's job.

Canvassing affords the project manager or proposals manager an opportunity to assess the estimating capabilities of all the individuals concerned. Any estimate which appears unrealistic or outrageous can be questioned on the spot, and many other details can be sorted out with the least possible fuss and delay. One type of question which must frequently be asked of the estimator takes the form: 'Here is a job said to require four man-weeks; can four men do it in one week, or must the job be spread over four weeks of elapsed time with only one person able to work on it?' The answers to such questions are clearly important in scheduling time and resources, of which more will be said in later chapters.

Manufacturing estimates with no drawings

Project estimating is carried out on a much broader scale than run-of-the-mill production work. In the absence of detailed information, larger work packages must be visualized. The only people capable of taking this broader view are the more senior members of the organization. Departmental managers often become involved, if not in making the estimates at least in approving them. It is almost certain, for example, that the production manager's input will be needed for project manufacturing estimates.

Production staff often need help in their project estimating task. The person collecting the estimates can often supply this help by translating the design specification into terms that the production people can understand (but care must be taken not to read anything into the specification which is not there). Similarities with past projects can be suggested and any artists' impressions or other sketches which may be available can be amplified by verbal description.

Suppose that a cost estimate is needed for a control unit. This is a box filled with instrumentation but detailed design has yet to take place and manufacturing drawings do not exist. Only one box of this special type is to be made, for use on a particular project. The only information on which a cost estimate can be based is an engineer's written design specification. This specification simply states the functional performance expected of the completed product in terms of its input and output parameters and its planned operating environment. If the estimator is very lucky, there might be a rough outline sketch of the box.

The estimating method might proceed along the following lines. First, a description of the proposed box is needed, with some idea of its contents. The design engineers must provide this information, because they are the only people at this stage who can possibly have any real idea what the final, detailed article will be like.

Once a description of the box has been set down it is usually possible to scan the archives to find a previous piece of work which bears some resemblance to the new job. Classification and coding of work and cost records can be a great help when it comes to making such a search. It might be found that no direct parallel exists but that one previous job was similar, but somewhat simpler than the present object of concern. 'How much simpler?' is the question which must now be asked. The design engineer might say that about 10 per cent more components will be needed this time, which gives a reasonable basis for a comparative estimate, provided that sufficient historical cost data can be found.

Estimating units

Generally speaking, while wages and their related standard cost rates change from year to year, the time needed to carry out any particular job by a given method will not. Work-hours are therefore regarded as the fundamental basis for estimates. Conversion from man-hours to money can only be regarded as a derivative, secondary process which is dependent on variable factors and other influences.

Comparative estimates for labour, therefore, should always be based on man-hours or other time units, and never on the costs pertaining at two or more different dates. Project estimates can never, of course, be expressed in fine units of time. Man-weeks or man-hours are the usual choices. Using anything less (man-minutes for example) would expose the cost estimator to the same trap as the scientist who carries out research using data and measurements accurate to no better than 1 or 2 per cent, but then has the temerity to express the final results using long strings of decimal places.

Personal estimating characteristics

Project cost estimating is not an exact science. Much of the process, particularly when estimating labour times, has to rely on the subjective judgement of individuals. If any ten people were to be asked separately to judge the time needed for a particular project task, it is hardly conceivable that ten identical answers would be received. Repeat this exercise with the same group of people for a number of different project tasks, and a pattern will doubtlessly emerge when the results are analysed. Some of those people will tend always to estimate on the low side. Others might give answers that are consistently high. The person collecting project cost estimates needs to be aware of this problem. In fact, just as it is possible to classify estimates according to confidence in their accuracy, so it is possible to classify the estimators themselves.

Optimistic estimators

As a general rule estimates for any work will more frequently be understated than overstated. Many people seem to be blessed with an unquenchable spirit of optimism when asked to predict completion times for any specific task. 'I can polish off that little job in three days', it is often claimed, but three weeks later only excuses have been produced. Without such optimism the world might be a much duller place in which to live and work, but the project manager's lot would be much easier.

An interesting feature of optimistic estimators is the way in which they allow their Cloud-cuckoo-land dreams to persist, even after seeing several jobs completed in double the time that they originally forecast. They continue to churn out estimates which are every bit as hopeful as the last, and appear quite unable to learn from previous experience. Engineers are perhaps the chief offenders in this respect, with draughtsmen running them a very close second. Fortunately the 'ill wind' proverb holds good, with the wind in this situation blowing to the good of the project manager. The source of consolation in analysing such estimates lies in the fact that they are at least consistent in their trend. In fact, shrewd project managers will come to learn by experience just how pronounced the trend is in their own particular company. Better still, they will be able to apportion error factors to particular individuals. A typical multiplication factor is 1.5: in other words it is often necessary to add about 50 per cent to the original estimates.

Pessimistic estimators

Occasionally another kind of individual is encountered who, unlike the optimist of more customary experience, can be relied upon to give overestimates for most tasks. This characteristic is not particularly common and, when seen, it might pay to investigate the underlying cause. Possibly the estimator lacks experience or is incompetent, although the typical symptom of estimating incompetence is random behaviour and not a consistent error trend.

The picture becomes clearer, if more unsavoury, when it is remembered that project estimates play a large part in determining total departmental budgets. Higher project estimates mean (if they are accepted) bigger budgets for costs and manpower, and thus expanding departments. This in turn adds to the status of the departmental heads. In these cases, therefore, 'E' stands not only for 'estimator' but also for 'empire builder'. Correction factors are possible, but action is more effective when it is aimed not at the estimates but at their originators.

Inconsistent estimators

The inconsistent estimator is the universal bane of the project manager's existence. Here we find a person who is seemingly incapable of estimating any job at all, giving answers that range over the whole spectrum from ridiculous pessimism to ludicrous optimism. The only characteristic consistently displayed is, in fact, inconsistency. Incompetence or inexperience suggest themselves as the most likely cause. Complacency could be another. Older people looking forward to retirement rather than promotion, and staff who were overlooked during the last round of promotions, can display these symptoms.

Unfortunately this category can manifest itself at departmental head level, the very people most frequently asked to provide estimates. Only time can solve this one.

Accurate estimators

It has to be allowed that there is a possibility, however remote, of finding a manager capable of providing estimates that are proved to be consistently accurate when the work actually takes place. This contingency is so remote that it can almost be discounted. When this rare phenomenon does occur it is apt to produce a very unsettling effect on the work-hardened project manager who has, through long experience, learned that it pays always to question every report received and never to take any estimate at its face value.

Making allowances

Why not try to educate the estimators? Prevention, after all, is better than cure. But the results of such a re-education programme must be unpredictable, with the effects varying from person to person, upsetting the previous equilibrium. In any case, all the estimators could be expected to slip back into their old ways eventually and, during the process, their estimating bias could lie anywhere on the scale between extreme optimism and pessimism. Arguing wastes time if nothing is achieved. Accept the situation as it exists and be grateful that it is at least predictable.

Here, then, is a picture of a project manager or proposals manager obtaining a set of estimates for a project, sitting down with a list of all the estimators who were involved, complete with the correction factor deemed appropriate for each individual, and then factoring the original estimates accordingly. Far-fetched? The value of this procedure has been proved in practice.

Estimates for material and equipment costs

Materials and the purchasing function are not often accorded the importance that they deserve in the context of project management. Expenditure on materials and bought-out services can easily exceed half the total cost of a typical industrial project. Failure to get materials on time is a common cause of delays and late project completion. Materials always need two types of estimates. For each task or work package these are as follows:

1 The total expected cost, including all delivery and other charges.
2 The total lead time, which is the time expected to elapse between starting the purchase order process and receiving the goods.

It might also be necessary to make estimates of other factors for operational purposes, for example the volume or weight of materials (information needed for storage and handling).

If detailed design has yet to be carried out, no parts lists, bills of materials or other schedules will exist from which to start the estimating process. Therefore the next best approach is to ask the engineers to prepare provisional lists of materials for each task. This may be impossible to carry out in detail, but the problem is not as difficult as it would first seem. In most work the engineers have a very good idea of the more significant and most expensive items that will have to be purchased. There might be special components, instruments, control gear, bearings, heavy weldments, castings, all depending of course on the type of project. Items such as these can account for a high proportion of the costs and are frequently those which take the longest time to obtain. In construction projects outline assumptions can be made for the types and quantities of bulk materials needed.

Foreknowledge of these main items of expense reduces the unknown area of estimating and therefore improves the estimating accuracy. If all the important items can be listed and priced, the remaining miscellaneous purchases can be estimated by intelligent guesswork. Records of past projects can be consulted to help assess the probable magnitude of the unknown element. If, for example, the known main components are going to account for 50 per cent of the total material costs, an error of 10 per cent in estimating the cost of the other materials would amount to only 5 per cent of the total. It is most important, however, to list items very carefully, ensuring that the job is done conscientiously and without significant omissions.

The purchasing department should always be involved, and estimates for prices and delivery times must be obtained through their efforts whenever possible. If the purchasing organization is not allowed to partake in preparing the detailed estimates, a real danger exists that when the time eventually comes to order the goods these will be obtained from the wrong suppliers at the wrong prices. It is far better if the big items of expense can be priced by quotations from the probable suppliers. The buyer can file all such quotations away in readiness for the time when the project becomes live. If the purchasing department is to be held down to a project materials budget, then it is only reasonable that it should play the leading role in producing the material estimates.

Materials estimating responsibility, therefore, lies in two areas. The engineers or design representatives must specify what materials are going to be used, and the purchasing department will be expected to find out how much they will cost and how long they will take to obtain.

Any estimate for materials is not complete unless all the costs of packing, transport, insurance, port duties, taxes and handling have been taken into account. The intending purchaser must be clear on what the price includes, and allowances must be made to take care of any services that are needed but not included in the quoted price.

Another cautionary word concerns the period of validity for quotations received from potential suppliers. Project cost estimates are often made many months – even years – before a contract is eventually awarded. Suppliers' quotations are typically valid for only 90 days or even less, so there could be a problem with the materials cost budget or the availability of goods when the time eventually arrives for the purchase orders to be placed.

The general purpose estimating form shown in Figure 5.2 allows space for simple materials estimating requirements, like those needed for a small manufacturing project. For larger projects, especially those involving international movements, a format such as that shown in Figure 5.3 would be more appropriate.

Below-the-line costs

When all the basic costs have been estimated, a line can be drawn under them and the total should amount to the estimated net cost of sales. There are, however, often costs which have to be considered and entered below that line.

Contingency allowances

A common source of estimating errors is the failure to appreciate that additional costs are bound to arise as the result of design errors, production mistakes, material or component failures and the like. The degree to which these contingencies are going to add to the project costs will depend on many factors, including the type of project, the general competency of the firm, the soundness (or otherwise) of the engineering concepts and so on.

Performance on previous projects should be a reliable pointer that can be used to decide just how much to allow on each new project to cover unforeseen circumstances. For a straightforward project, not entailing an inordinate degree of risk, an allowance set at 5 per cent of the above-the-line costs might be adequate.

The scope for adding an adequate contingency allowance will be restricted if there is high price competition from the market. If the perceived risk suggests the need for a very high contingency allowance, perhaps the company should reconsider whether or not to tender at all.

Cost escalation

Every year wages and salaries increase, raw materials and bought-out components tend to cost more, transport becomes more expensive and plant and buildings absorb more money. All these increases correspond to the familiar decrease in the real value of money which is termed 'inflation'. This decay appears to be inevitable, and the rate is usually fairly predictable in the short

Cost code	Description	Specn. No. (if known)	Proposed supplier	Unit	Unit cost FOB	Quoted currency	Exchange rate used	Converted FOB cost	Qty	Project FOB cost	Ship mode	Freight cost	Taxes/ duties	Delivered cost

COST ESTIMATE FOR MATERIALS AND PURCHASED EQUIPMENT

Estimate for:

Project number or sales reference:

Compiled by:

Estimate number:
Case:
Date:
Page   of

Total delivered materials and equipment costs this page ⟶

Figure 5.3   Cost estimating form for purchased goods on a capital project

term. In a country where the rate of inflation is 10 per cent, a project that was accurately estimated in 2000 to cost $5m (say) might cost an extra million dollars if its start were to be delayed for two years.

Unfortunately, cost inflation rates are not easy to predict over the long term, because they are subject to a range of political, environmental and economic factors. However, a cost escalation allowance based on the best possible prediction should be made for any project whose duration is expected significantly to exceed one year. The rate chosen by the estimator for below-the-line cost escalation allowances might have to be negotiated and agreed with the customer, for example in defence or other contracts to be carried out for a national government.

The conditions of contract may allow the contractor to claim a price increase in the event of specified cost escalation events that are beyond its control (for example a national industry wage award), but that is a different case from including escalation in quoted rates and prices as a below-the-line allowance.

Using a validity time limit to reduce cost escalation risk

The actual starting date for a project can often be delayed for a considerable time after the contractor submits a fixed price proposal. Such delays are common. Factors such as internal committee decisions, internal committee indecision, legal considerations, local authority planning requirements, environmental pressures, political interference, confirmation of final technical details and arranging a financing package can easily add many months or years to the start date and subsequent timescale of a project. The contracting company will usually safeguard itself against this risk by placing a time limit on the validity of rates or prices quoted in the tender.

Provisional sums

It often happens, particularly in construction contracts, that the contractor foresees the possibility of additional work that might arise if particular difficulties are encountered when work actually starts. For example, a client may specify that materials are to be salvaged from a building during demolition work, to be reused in the new construction. The contractor might wish to reserve its position by including a provisional sum, to be added to the project price in the event that the salvaged materials prove unsuitable for reuse. It is not unusual for a project quotation to include more than one provisional sum, covering several quite different eventualities.

Foreign currencies

Most large projects involve transactions in currencies other than their own national currency. This can give rise to uncertainty and risk when the exchange rates vary. Some mitigation of this effect can be achieved if the contract includes safeguards or if all quotations can be made and obtained in the home currency. Otherwise, it is a matter of skill, judgement and foresight.

Common practice in project cost estimating is to nominate one currency as the control currency for the project and then to convert all estimated costs into that currency using carefully chosen exchange rates. Although contractors would normally choose their home currency, projects may have to be quoted in foreign currencies if the terms of tendering so demand, and if the potential client insists.

Whether or not the contractor wishes to disclose the exchange rates used in reaching the final cost estimates, the rates used for all conversions must be shown clearly on the internally circulated estimating forms.

Reviewing the cost estimates

When all the detailed estimates have been collected it should, theoretically, be possible to add them all up and pronounce a forecast of the total project cost. When this stage has been reached, however, it is never a bad plan to stand well back for a while and view the picture from a wider angle. In particular, try converting the figures for labour times into man-years. Suppose that the engineering design work needed for a project appears to need 8750 man-hours (or, perhaps, 250 man-weeks, according to the estimating units used). Taking 1750 man-hours or 50 man-weeks as being roughly equivalent to a man-year, rapid division of the estimate immediately shows that five man-years must be spent to complete the project design. Now assume that all the design is scheduled to be finished in the first six months of the programme. This could be viewed (simplistically) as a requirement of ten engineers for six months.

The manager starting this project might experience a rude awakening on referring to records of past projects. These might well show that projects of similar size and complexity took not ten engineers for six months, but expenditure equivalent to ten engineers for a whole year. An apparent error of five man-years exists somewhere. This is, in any language, a king-sized problem. Part of its cause could be the failure of estimators to allow for that part of engineering design which is sometimes called 'after-issue', which means making corrections, incorporating unfunded modifications, answering engineering queries from the workforce or the customer, writing reports and putting records into archives.

It goes without saying that cost estimates for a project are extremely important. Any serious error could prove disastrous for the contractor – and for the customer if it leads the contractor into financial difficulties. Estimates should, therefore, always be checked as far as possible by a competent person who is independent of the estimate compiler. Comparisons with actual cost totals for past projects (for all materials and labour – not just engineering design) are valuable in checking that the new project cost estimate at least appears to be in the right league.

6

Planning

In project management terminology, some planners recognize that the words 'plan' and 'schedule' can have different meanings.

A plan is the listing or visual display that results when all project activities have been subjected to estimating, logical sequencing and time analysis. For all practical purposes, some form of network analysis is usually the preferred method for preparing a plan, but bar charts provide better visual aids and can be more effective for communicating plans to project personnel.

A schedule is obtained by doing additional work on the initial plan, so that resources needed to carry out all the project activities are taken into account. In other words, a schedule is the working document that results from matching the initial plan to the organization's available resources. Scheduling is dealt with in Chapter 7.

Bar charts

Bar charts derive from Gantt charts, named after their originator, the American industrial engineer Henry Gantt (1861–1919). They have long been in widespread use, and they continue to be very valuable planning aids. Bar charts are not only easy to draw or construct and interpret but are also readily adaptable to a great variety of planning requirements. The visual impact of a well-drawn bar chart can be a powerful aid to controlling a project.

Bar charts are still preferred to other methods in many executives' offices, on project sites and in factories. All levels of supervision and management find them convenient as day-to-day control tools. Even when projects have been planned with more advanced computer techniques, the same computer systems are often used to translate the schedules into bar charts for day-to-day use.

Bar charts can be assembled on wall-mounted boards, using proprietary kits (although these are now far less common because of the alternatives available using computer systems). These proprietary charts use strips of material, which can be colour coded, and which can be moved about to adjust the schedule as required. Coded adjustable bar charts are the simplest method for scheduling resources on very small projects.

Timescale

Bar charts are drawn or constructed on a scale where the horizontal axis is directly proportional to time. Days, months, years or other units are used, chosen to suit the duration of the project. Each horizontal bar represents a project task, its length scaled according to its expected duration. The name or description of each job is written on the same row, at the left-hand edge of the chart.

A bar chart case study: the furniture project

Eaton Sitright Limited is a company that manufactures good quality furniture for sale to homes and offices. The company wishes to introduce a new desk and chair design to its standard range and has started a project to design and make a small prototype batch for consumer appraisal and testing. The furniture will be steel framed, and the desk is to be provided with one drawer. Figure 6.1 lists the main tasks for this project. The jobs are listed in separate chronological order for the chair, and for the desk. The general tasks at the foot of the list apply to the whole project. No attempt has been made in this tabulation to state any relationship between the tasks, but the company's planner can bear these in mind and avoid logical errors when the plans are made.

Task number	Task description	Duration (days)
	Chair	
01	Anatomical study for chair	15
02	Design chair	5
03	Buy materials for chair seat	6
04	Make chair seat	3
05	Buy chair castors	5
06	Buy steel for chair frame	10
07	Make chair frame	3
08	Paint chair frame	2
09	Assemble chair	1
10	Apply final finishes to chair	2
	Desk	
11	Design desk	10
12	Buy steel for desk frame	10
13	Make desk frame	5
14	Paint desk frame	2
15	Buy wood and fittings for desk	5
16	Make desk drawer	6
17	Make desk top	1
18	Assemble desk	1
19	Apply final finishes to desk	2
	General activities	
20	Decide paint colours	10
21	Buy paint and varnish	8
22	Final project evaluation	5

Figure 6.1 Task list for desk and chair project

Figure 6.2 is the resulting bar chart. The planner has been careful not to schedule any job before it can actually take place. For example, the paint colours must be decided before the paint can be purchased. No painting task can start before the relevant article has been manufactured and the paint has been purchased. Although the chart cannot show these relationships, these can be dealt with mentally on this simple project. With a larger project, however, there would be considerable risk of producing a chart containing some logical impossibilities.

Vertical link lines can be added to bar charts to show constraints between jobs. Figure 6.3 is a linked version of the bar chart of Figure 6.2. This clearly shows, for example, that the chair design

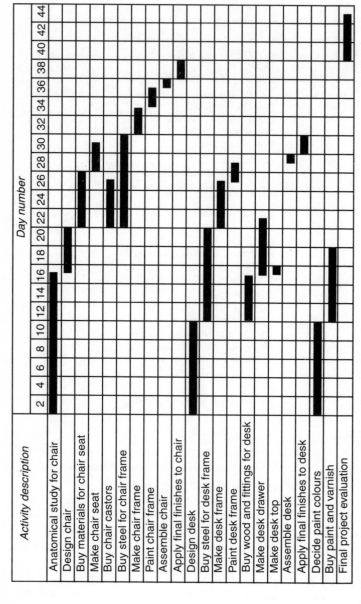

Figure 6.2 Bar chart for desk and chair project

94

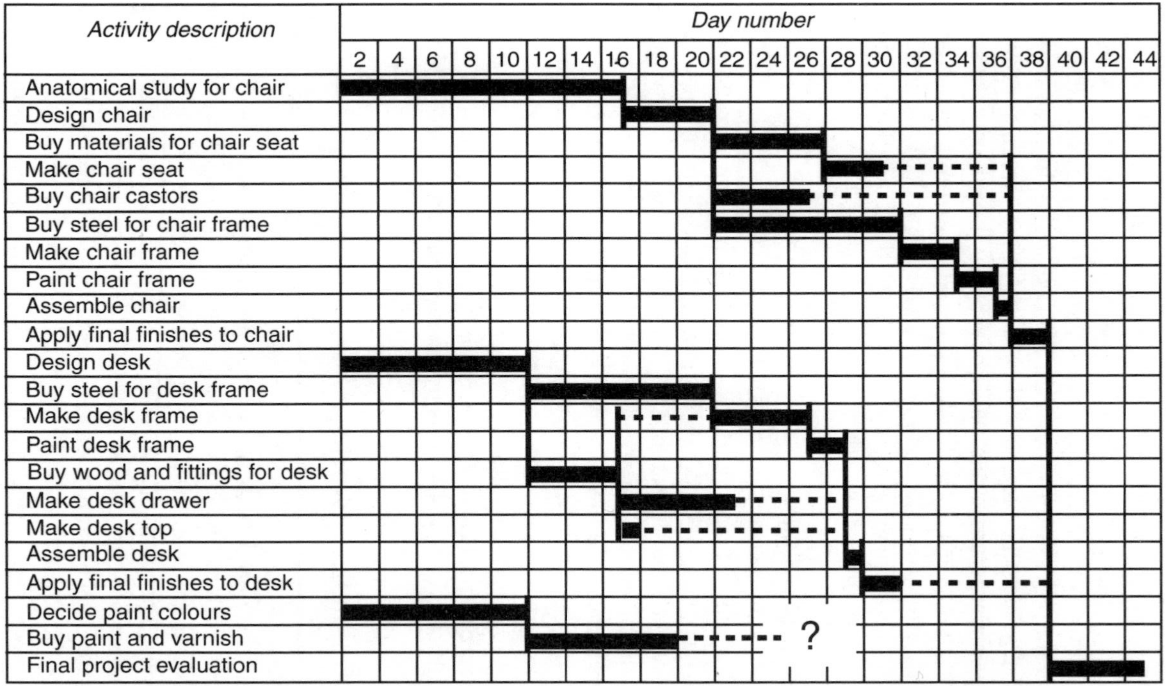
Activity description
Day number
2
4
6
8
10
12
14
16
18
20
22
24
26
28
30
32
34
36
38
40
42
44
Anatomical study for chair
Design chair
Buy materials for chair seat
Make chair seat
Buy chair castors
Buy steel for chair frame
Make chair frame
Paint chair frame
Assemble chair
Apply final finishes to chair
Design desk
Buy steel for desk frame
Make desk frame
Paint desk frame
Buy wood and fittings for desk
Make desk drawer
Make desk top
Assemble desk
Apply final finishes to desk
Decide paint colours
Buy paint and varnish
Final project evaluation
?

Figure 6.3 Linked bar chart for desk and chair project

cannot start before the anatomical study has been completed. Even for this simple project, however, the linked bar chart cannot show every task dependency. It would be difficult to draw the links from 'Buy paint and varnish' to the starts of the two painting jobs without producing crossovers and some confusion (although, in this simple case, these particular crossovers could be eliminated by rearranging the sequence of tasks). Many project management computer programs are capable of plotting linked bar charts, but the results are usually difficult or impossible to interpret.

This furniture project will be revisited later in this chapter to see how much more effective it would be for the Eaton Sitright company to plan the work with network analysis.

Bar chart limitations

The inability of bar charts to depict clearly the dependencies between different tasks has already been demonstrated. Bar charts have other limitations. Although it is possible to schedule more than 100 jobs on an adjustable bar chart, rescheduling is a different story. Setting a complex plan up in the first place might take a few working days or a week. Adjusting it subsequently to keep in step with changes might prove impossible.

The visual effectiveness of a chart is lost when too many colour codes are introduced, or when there are so many tasks shown that it is difficult to trace their positions along the rows and columns.

Critical path networks

When compared with bar charts (including linked bar charts), critical path networks provide the more powerful notation needed to show all the logical interdependencies between different jobs. The planner can ensure, for example, that bricklaying will never be scheduled to start before its supporting foundations are ready. Such errors are easily possible with complex bar charts, where the constraints cannot all be shown or remembered.

Another great strength of networks is that they allow priorities to be quantified, based on an analysis of all the task duration estimates. Those tasks that cannot be delayed without endangering project completion on time are identified as critical, and all other tasks can be ranked according to their degree of criticality.

Networks cannot, by themselves, be used for resource scheduling. In this respect bar charts are superior and easier to understand, provided that the number of activities is very small. However, networks (because they assign time-based priorities and highlight critical jobs) make a vital contribution to the resource scheduling process. Resource scheduling will be described in Chapter 7.

Network notation is particularly suited to computer input and there are many available software packages, some of which combine very powerful resource scheduling capabilities.

The benefits to be derived from drawing a network are in themselves often worthwhile, even if no duration estimates are made, no time analysis takes place and the network is not used to control subsequent progress. Networking encourages a logical progression of thinking and planning. In fact a network planning meeting can be regarded as a productive form of brainstorming. Not only does the notation allow expression of all inter-activity dependencies and relationships, but there is also the important possibility that activities may be brought to light which might otherwise have been excluded from schedules, estimates and (most important) pricing.

The different network notation systems

Several network systems emerged during the second half of the twentieth century, but these all fit within one or other of two principal groups, determined by the method of notation:

1 Activity-on-arrow system, often called arrow networks or ADM networks (short for arrow diagram).
2 Precedence networks, also known as activity-on-node or PDM networks (short for precedence diagram).

I use both methods (arrow networks for initial sketching at brainstorming meetings and precedence networks for computer applications). Arrow networks are faster and easier to draw than precedence networks, saving valuable time at initial planning meetings, which are invariably attended by busy senior people. I have been told, however, that it is possible to 'draw' relatively simple precedence networks at brainstorming sessions by sticking 3M Post-it Notes on a flip chart or roll of paper to represent the activities. Arrow networks will be described briefly in this chapter, but most of the examples will be given using the precedence system.

When a planner prefers to draw the first draft network in arrow notation, it is a very simple matter to convert to precedence notation later if the plan is going to be processed by a computer. Precedence logic, although not as well suited as arrow for hand sketching, is particularly easy to draw and edit on the computer screen.

Critical path networks using arrow diagrams

All significant definitions given here are repeated in the precedence diagram section, allowing readers to skip this arrow section if they wish.

Activities and events

Figure 6.4 shows a very simple arrow diagram. Each circle denotes a project event, such as the start of work or the completion of a task. The arrow joining any two events represents the activity or task that must take place before the second event can be declared as achieved. In Figure 6.4 there are, therefore, six activities linking six events (ignore the dotted arrow for the time being).

Activity arrows and indeed all network diagrams are by convention drawn so that work progresses from left to right. The diagrams are not usually drawn to scale and the length of arrows and spacing of events has no significance whatsoever.

The numbers in the event circles are there simply to label the events: they allow the events and their associated activities to be referred to without ambiguity. Thus the arrow from event 1 to event 2 can be described as activity 1 to 2. This labelling is con-

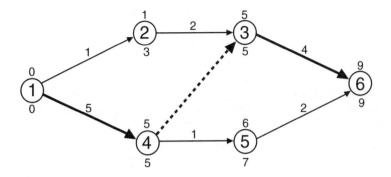

Figure 6.4 An activity-on-arrow network diagram

venient for all arrow networks and essential for any network which is to be processed by a computer (although network programs capable of processing arrow networks are, regrettably, practically extinct).

The logical significance of the diagram in Figure 6.4 is that each event cannot be considered achieved until the activity or activities leading into it have been finished. Only then, and not before, can activities immediately following the event be started.

The dotted arrow in Figure 6.4 is a dummy activity. Dummy activities (always called dummies for short) do not represent actual work and practically always have zero duration. Rather, they denote a constraint or line of dependence between different activities. In this case, therefore, the start of activity 3 to 6 is dependent not only upon completion of activity 2 to 3, but it must also await completion of activity 1 to 4. Alternatively expressed, activity 3 to 6 cannot start until events 3 and 4 have both been achieved.

In practice, each arrow on a real project network would have its task name or description written along the length of the arrow. Descriptions are usually kept short, through lack of space on the diagram (and, subsequently, in the appropriate computer data field).

Time analysis

Numbers have been written above the activity arrows in Figure 6.4 to show their estimated durations. The units used are always chosen by the planner as being the most suitable for the project. Once chosen, the same time units must be used consistently throughout any network. Assume that the numbers in this illustration are weeks. These estimates are strictly for duration only, which means elapsed time, not necessarily the work content. In fact, for some 'activities' (such as procurement lead times) there might be no work content for the project staff at all.

The first purpose of time analysis is to determine the shortest possible time in which a project can be completed, taking into account all the logical constraints and activity duration estimates. However, it is not usual to take possible shortage of resources into account at this stage because that problem can be resolved at a later stage (see Chapter 7).

Time analysis also performs the vital function of determining which activities should be given the most priority. This is achieved by calculating a quantity called float, which is the amount by which any activity can be allowed to slip past its earliest possible start date without delaying the whole project. This concept will become clearer as this chapter proceeds.

The forward pass

In the project network of Figure 6.4, the earliest project duration possible has been calculated by adding the activity duration estimates along the arrows from left to right. This is always the first step in the full time analysis of any network and is known as the 'forward pass'.

The forward pass additions have been somewhat complicated in this case because there is more than one possible path through the network. The sums will depend on which path is followed. The earliest possible completion time for event 3, for instance, might seem to be 1 + 2 = 3, if the path through events 1, 2 and 3 is taken. Completion of event 3 cannot be achieved, however, until event 4 has also been achieved, because of the link through the dummy. It so happens that the path through the dummy is the longer of the two possible paths and that must, therefore, determine the earliest possible time for the achievement of event 3. The earliest possible time for event 3 is, therefore, the end of week 5. That also means that the earliest possible start time for activity 3 to 6 is the end of week 5.

Thus the earliest possible time for any event (and the earliest possible start time for its succeeding activity) is found by adding the estimated durations of all preceding activities along the path that produces the greatest time. By following this procedure through the network to the end of the project at event 6 it emerges that the earliest possible estimated project completion time is nine weeks.

The backward pass
Now consider event 5 in Figure 6.4. Its earliest possible achievement time is the end of week 6, three weeks before the earliest possible time for finishing the project at event 6. It is clear that activity 5 to 6, which is only expected to last for two weeks, could be delayed for up to one week without upsetting the overall timescale. In other words, although the earliest possible achievement time for event 5 is week 6, its latest permissible achievement time is week 7. This result can be indicated on the arrow diagram by writing the latest permissible time underneath the event circle. The result is found this time, not by addition from left to right along the arrows, but in the opposite way by subtracting the estimated durations of activities from right to left (9 − 2 = 7 for event 5).

This subtraction exercise can be repeated throughout the network, writing the latest permissible times below all the event circles. Where more than one path exists, the longest must always be chosen so that the result after subtraction gives the smallest remainder. This is illustrated at event 4, where the correct subtraction route lies through the dummy.

Although the earliest and latest times are written above and below the event circles, they can also be applied to the activities leading into and out of the events. Thus, for example, activity 5 to 6 has:

- duration: 2 weeks
- earliest possible start: end of week 6 (beginning of week 7)
- earliest possible finish (6 + 2): end of week 8
- latest permissible finish: end of week 9
- total float (9 − 8): 1 week.

Float and the critical path

The term 'float' indicates the amount of leeway available for starting and finishing an activity without the project end date being affected. Total float is the difference between the earliest and latest times for any activity. There are other categories of float: these are explained in Chapter 7 but can be ignored for the purposes of the examples in this chapter.

When all the earliest possible and latest permissible times have been added to the diagram, there will always be at least one chain of events where the earliest and latest times are the same, indicating zero float. These events are critical to the successful achievement of the whole project within its earliest possible time. The route joining these events is not surprisingly termed the 'critical path'. Although all activities may be important, it is the critical activities that must claim priority for scarce resources and management attention.

Precedence diagrams

This section repeats some of the text from the previous section for the benefit of readers who decided to skip the account of arrow networks.

A precedence diagram must be constructed with careful thought to ensure that it shows as accurately as possible the logical relationships and interdependencies of each activity or task with all the others in the project. For this reason networks are sometimes called logic diagrams.

Activities

Figure 6.5 shows the notation commonly used for an activity in precedence notation and Figure 6.6 is the precedence equivalent of the arrow diagram in Figure 6.4. The numbers in brackets in each activity box in Figure 6.6 indicate the equivalent arrows in Figure 6.4.

The flow of work in any network diagram is from left to right. Precedence diagrams are not usually drawn to scale and the length of links or size of the activity boxes have no significance whatsoever. Every activity is given a unique identification num-

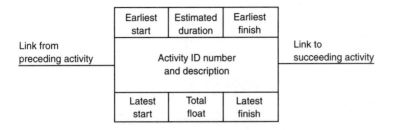

Figure 6.5   An activity in precedence notation

ber, often referred to as its ID code. These codes are required for computer processing. ID codes can range from small serial numbers to complex alphanumeric codes containing ten or even more characters (depending on the size and complexity of the networks, the nature of the projects being planned and the capabilities of the computer software).

All the activities comprising a project are joined by arrows which, unlike those in arrow diagrams, simply represent constraints or links. In fact, because we draw all arrows from left to right, we usually leave out the arrowheads.

Dummy activities are activities that denote no work but are included in a network to create correct logic by showing links between dependent activities. Dummy activities are usually unnecessary in precedence networks because, in fact, all the logical links are dummies. However, dummy activities can be useful as interface activities common to two or more different subnetworks in a complex work breakdown arrangement (outside the scope of this book). It is also convenient to create artificial start and finish activities for a precedence network: otherwise there will be a tendency for networks to have several starts and several finishes, which will be found untidy for time analysis and for computer processing. This has been done in Figure 6.6, where activities 1 and 8 are effectively dummy activities.

Complex constraints

Precedence notation allows more freedom to express complex inter-activity relationships than the arrow method. However,

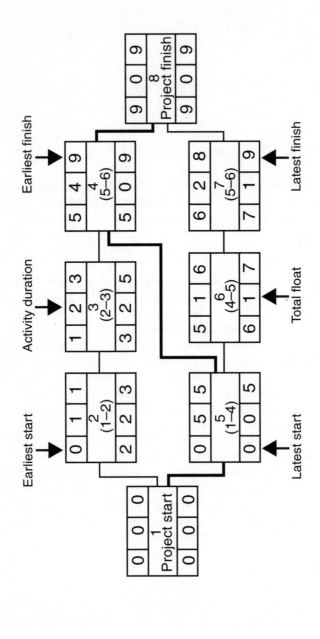

Figure 6.6 A precedence network diagram

This is the precedence version of the arrow network shown in Figure 6.4.

only very simple sequential (finish-to-start) relationships are used in the examples given here. These simple links are by far the most commonly used. Many people avoid using the more complex links, but the options are shown in Figure 6.7 for those who might need to use them.

Time analysis of precedence networks

The units used for estimated activity durations are chosen by the planner as being the most suitable for the project. Once chosen, the same time units must be used consistently throughout any network. Assume that the numbers in Figure 6.6 are weeks. These estimates are for duration only, which means elapsed time, not necessarily the work content. In fact, for some 'activities' (such as procurement lead times) there might be no work content for the project staff at all.

The first purpose of time analysis is to determine the shortest possible time in which a project can be completed, taking into account all the logical constraints and activity duration estimates. However, it is not usual to take possible shortage of resources into account at this stage because that problem is resolved at a later stage (see Chapter 7).

Time analysis also performs the vital function of determining which activities should be given the most priority. This is achieved by calculating a quantity called float, which is the amount by which any activity can be allowed to slip past its earliest possible start date without delaying the whole project. This concept will become clearer as this chapter proceeds.

The forward pass

In the project network of Figure 6.6, the earliest project duration possible has been calculated by adding activity duration estimates along the various paths, through the links, passing from left to right.

As there is more than one possible path through the network, the totals will obviously depend on which path is followed. The earliest possible start time for activity 4, for instance, would seem to be $0 + 1 + 2 = 3$ (the end of week 3) if the path through activities 1, 2 and 3 is taken. However, activity 4 cannot start until the end of week 5, because it is constrained by the longer path through activities 1 and 5.

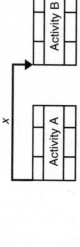

(a) Finish-to-start. Activity *B* cannot start until *x* network time units after the finish of Activity *A*. Most constraints are of this type, but *x* is usually zero.

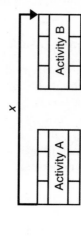

(b) Start-to-start. Activity *B* cannot start until *x* network time units after the start of Activity *A*.

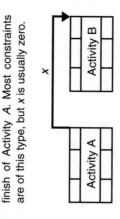

(c) Finish-to-finish. Activity *B* cannot be finished until *x* network time units after the finish of Activity *A*.

(d) Start-to-finish. Activity *B* cannot be finished until *x* network time units after the start of Activity *A*.

Figure 6.7 Complex constraints possible with precedence notation

106

Thus the earliest possible start time for any activity is found by adding the times of all preceding activities along the longest path in the network. By following this procedure through the network to the end of the project at activity 8 it emerges that the earliest possible estimated project duration is nine weeks.

The backward pass
Now consider activity 7 in Figure 6.6. Its earliest possible start time is the end of week 6, three weeks before the earliest possible time for finishing the project at activity 8. It is clear that activity 7, which is only expected to last for two weeks, could be delayed for up to one week without upsetting the overall timescale. This result can be indicated on the activity box by writing the latest permissible start time in its bottom left-hand corner. The result is found this time, not by addition from left to right along the arrows, but in the opposite way by subtraction from right to left $(9 - 2 = 7$ for activity 7). The other quantities along the bottom of this activity box can now be filled in, namely the float of one week and the activity's latest permissible finish date (end of week 9).

This subtraction exercise can be repeated throughout the network, writing the latest permissible times and float in all the activity boxes. Where more than one path exists, the longest must be chosen so that the result after subtraction gives the smallest remainder. This is illustrated at activity 5, for instance, where the correct subtraction route lies through activities 8 and 4.

Float and the critical path
The term 'float' indicates the amount of leeway available for starting and finishing an activity without affecting the project end date. Total float is the difference between the earliest and latest times for any activity. There are other categories of float: these are explained in Chapter 7 but can be ignored for the purposes of the examples in this chapter.

When all the earliest possible and latest permissible times have been added to the diagram, there will always be at least one chain of events where the earliest and latest times are the same, indicating zero float. These events are critical to the successful achievement of the whole project within its earliest possible time. The route joining these events is not surprisingly termed the 'critical path'. Although all activities may be important, it is the critical activities that must claim priority for scarce resources and management attention.

Case study: the gantry project

A slightly more substantial project example will show how network logic and critical path calculation work in practice.

Project explanation

Figure 6.8 shows a steel gantry that has to be set up on the side of a steep hill. The requirements of this small project are quite simple, but one or two points have to be borne in mind about the order in which the work is to be carried out.

The first step in erecting this gantry must be to mark out the site and prepare the foundations. Assume that all other preparations, including the delivery of plant and materials to site, have already been carried out. Because of the asymmetry the two tower foundations differ in size, because foundation B will bear more weight than the other. Tower B has to be placed on a prefabricated plinth in order to raise it to the same height as tower A. A final levelling adjustment must be made at base A after the plinth has been

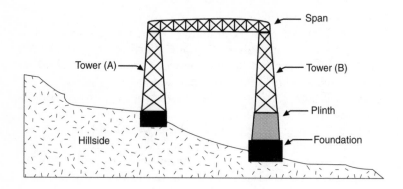

Figure 6.8   The gantry project

erected for B, and this is to be done by taking a theodolite sighting from the plinth top. All these special requirements are reflected in the project network diagram. All estimates and times are in days for this project.

Network diagram for the gantry project

Figure 6.9 shows the network diagram for the gantry project. This is presented in two versions, as an arrow diagram (upper portion) and as a precedence network. The remainder of this section will refer only to the precedence version.

The link from activity 10 to activity 5 has been added to show that base A cannot be levelled until the plinth has been erected at B. Activities 4 and 9 are both waiting times, while concrete cures. This is hardly work or activity and the precedence notation would, in fact, allow these activities to be shown simply by placing links from 3 to 5 and 8 to 10 and giving these links duration values. However, it is always safer to insert activities in the network if paper and computer space allows, because the logic and the planner's intentions are then more clearly recorded and made visible. Such 'visibility' will be beneficial during subsequent network checking and in the interpretation of reports from the computer.

Time analysis of the gantry project network

The forward pass
Addition of the duration estimates, working from left to right through the network, gives the earliest activity start and finish times. Where there are alternative paths, with more than one immediate predecessor to an activity, the longest path must determine the earliest possible start time for the activity. This is evident at activities 5 and 12 in Figure 6.9. The earliest possible completion date for this project is seen to be at the end of day 26.

The backward pass
The critical path in the gantry project has been found, as in the earlier examples of Figures 6.4 and 6.6, by subtracting activity durations through the network paths from right to left. The critical path in Figure 6.9 is seen to run through activities 1, 7, 8, 9, 10, 5, 6

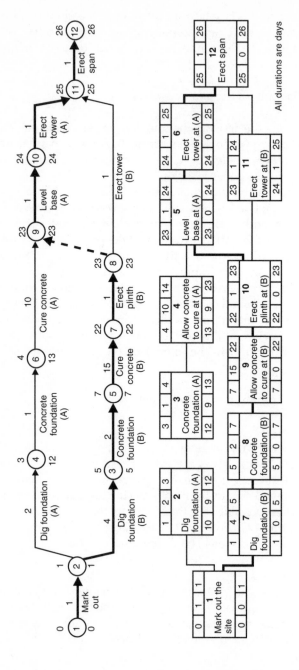

Figure 6.9 Gantry project network diagram

and 12. All activities on this path are critical, and a delay to any one of them must delay project completion.

Summary of time analysis results for the gantry project
The time analysis results from the gantry project are shown in Figure 6.10, tabulated as they might emerge from a simple computer calculation. If the times in this table are desired as calendar dates (they usually will be) a calendar must obviously be consulted for the conversion. Non-working days such as weekends and public holidays must be taken out. These chores are avoided when a computer is used.

Activity identifier	Activity description	Duration (days)	Earliest start	Earliest finish	Latest start	Latest finish	Total float
1	Mark out the site	1	0	1	0	1	0
2	Dig foundation for tower A	2	1	3	10	12	9
3	Concrete foundation A	1	3	4	12	13	9
4	Allow concrete to cure at A	10	4	14	13	23	9
7	Dig foundation for tower B	4	1	5	1	5	0
8	Concrete foundation B	2	5	7	5	7	0
9	Allow concrete to cure at B	15	7	22	7	22	0
10	Erect plinth at B	1	22	23	22	23	0
—	Dummy (arrow diagram only)	0	—	—	—	—	—
11	Erect tower B	1	23	24	24	25	1
5	Adjust base level at A	1	23	24	23	24	0
6	Erect tower A	1	24	25	24	25	0
12	Erect the span	1	25	26	25	26	0

Figure 6.10   Gantry project time analysis

Planning the furniture project by critical path network

Earlier in this chapter it was shown that bar charts are very limited in their ability to show the constraints between interdependent activities. The linked bar chart in Figure 6.3 could not show all the links clearly, even for the simple furniture project carried out by the Eaton Sitright company.

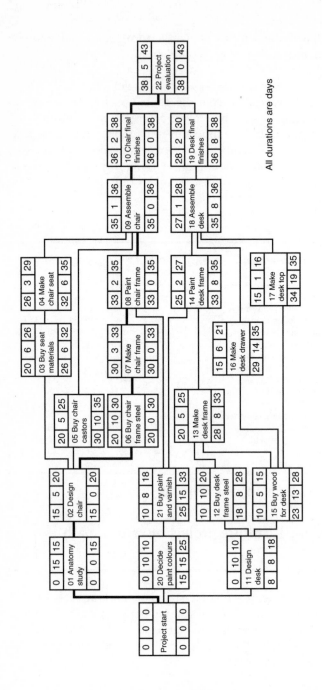

All durations are days

Figure 6.11 Precedence network diagram for the desk and chair project

Figure 6.11 shows how the furniture project plan looks as a precedence diagram. At first sight this is a little difficult to follow, but that is partly the price paid for having to cram the diagram into a small space so that it would fit the page in this book. The critical path is highlighted by the bold lines.

Activity identifier	Activity description	Duration (days)	Earliest start	Latest start	Earliest finish	Latest finish	Total float
01	Anatomical study for chair	15	0	0	15	15	0
02	Design chair	5	15	15	20	20	0
03	Buy materials for chair seat	6	20	26	26	32	6
04	Make chair seat	3	26	32	29	35	6
05	Buy chair castors	5	20	30	25	35	10
06	Buy steel for chair frame	10	20	20	30	30	0
07	Make chair frame	3	30	30	33	33	0
08	Paint chair frame	2	33	33	35	35	0
09	Assemble chair	1	35	35	36	36	0
10	Apply final finishes to chair	2	36	36	38	38	0
11	Design desk	10	0	8	10	18	8
12	Buy steel for desk frame	10	10	18	20	28	8
13	Make desk frame	5	20	28	25	33	8
14	Paint desk frame	2	25	33	27	35	8
15	Buy wood and fittings for desk	5	10	23	15	28	13
16	Make desk drawer	6	15	29	21	35	14
17	Make desk top	1	15	34	16	35	19
18	Assemble desk	1	27	35	28	36	8
19	Apply final finishes to desk	2	28	36	30	38	8
20	Decide paint colours	10	0	15	10	25	15
21	Buy paint and varnish	8	10	25	18	33	15
22	Final project evaluation	5	38	38	43	43	0

Figure 6.12   Desk and chair project time analysis

Figure 6.12 shows results of time analysis. Once the project start date has been established, all the numbers can be converted to calendar dates, with holidays and weekends allowed for. The resulting table should be of far more use to the manager of this project than any bar chart because it is not necessary to read the chart scale, and the relative priorities of the different tasks are clearly stated in terms of their total float.

Level of detail in network diagrams

A question often facing planners new to the art is 'How much detail should we show in the network?' In other words, which activities should be included in the network and which should be left out or combined with others?

To some extent this depends on the size of the project, the project duration, the size of the duration units chosen, the amount of detailed knowledge available and the purpose of the network. A very detailed project network containing 10 000 activities might sound very impressive, but smaller networks are more manageable. Also, very big single project networks can prove tiresome (to say the least) when they have to be considered along with plans for other projects in multiproject scheduling systems.

Guidelines

There are several guidelines that apply to the level of detail which should be shown in project network diagrams.

Activities with relatively very short durations
It is probably wise to avoid showing jobs as separate activities if their durations amount only to a very small fraction of the expected project timescale, especially if they do not require resources. Of course, these activities cannot be ignored, but they can be included in the network as parts of other activities.

An example might be the preparation of a group of drawings, where a single activity 'detail and check subassembly X' would be shown rather than including a separate activity for detailing every drawing, and another set of activities for checking them.

In a project lasting only a few weeks (for example the overhaul and maintenance of an electricity generating station during a planned period of shutdown) it would be reasonable to use network planning units of days or fractions of days, and to include activities lasting only half a day. For projects lasting several years, the planning units might be weeks, with very few activities included that have less than one week's duration.

As with all rules there are exceptions. Some activities with very short durations might be so important that they must be included (for example an activity for obtaining authorization or approval before subsequent work can proceed).

Level of detail in relation to task responsibility

It can be argued sensibly that a network path should be broken to include a new activity whenever the action moves from one department or organization to another – in other words where the responsibility for work changes. In the days when practically everyone used arrow networks this concept was easy to define: a new event should be created whenever responsibility progressed from one manager to another (or from one department to another).

A useful guide is to remember that the ultimate purpose of the network is to allow the project work to be scheduled and controlled. In due course, work-to-do lists for different managers will be generated from the network. The network must contain all the jobs needed for these lists. This means that:

- no network activity should be so large that it cannot be assigned for the principal control of one, and only one, department or manager;

- activities must correspond to actions that have a clearly definable start and finish; and

- the interval between the start and finish of any activity should not be too long compared with the project timescale, so that fairly frequent monitoring against planned events can take place.

A network that is sufficiently detailed will enable the following types of events to be identified, planned and monitored or measured:

1 Work authorization, either as an internal works order or as the receipt of a customer order or contract.

2 Financial authorizations from the customer (especially where these might risk work hold-ups during the course of the project).

3 Local authority planning application and consent.

4   The start and finish of design for any subassembly. If the duration of the design task is longer than two or three weeks it might be advisable to define separate, shorter activities corresponding to design phases.

5   Release of completed drawings for production or construction (probably grouped in subassemblies or work packages rather than attempting to plan for every individual small drawing).

6   The start of purchasing activity for each subassembly or work package, signified by the engineering issue of a bill of material, purchase specification or advance release of information for items which are known to have long delivery times.

7   Issue of invitations-to-tender or purchase enquiries.

8   Receipt and analysis of bids.

9   Following on from 6, 7 and 8, the issue of a purchase order with a supplier or subcontractor (again at the level of work packages and subassemblies and major items rather than small individual purchases).

10   Material deliveries, often meaning the event when the last item needed to complete the materials for a particular work package (or for a single item of capital equipment) is received on site or at the factory. For international projects, this delivery point may be to a ship or to an aircraft, with subsequent transit time shown as a separate, consecutive activity (when the change of responsibility rule applies, because responsibility transfers from the supplier to the carrier or freight forwarding agent).

11   The starts and completions of manufacturing stages (in large projects usually only looking at the entries into and exits from production control responsibility, and again considering work packages or subassemblies rather than individual small parts).

12   The starts and finishes of construction subcontracts, and important intermediate events in such subcontracts (see the section 'Milestones' below).

13 Handover activities for completed work packages. This would include activities for handing over the finished project, or substantial parts of it, to the customer but would also ensure that associated items such as maintenance and operating manuals were itemized separately in the network plan.

These are, of course, only guidelines. The list is neither mandatory nor complete.

Level of detail in relation to activity costs
Some cost control methods are described later in this book but certain aspects of cost reporting and control will be impossible if sufficient attention is not given to certain activities when the network diagram is prepared.

It is possible to assign a cost to an activity, such as the purchase of materials. If an activity is included on the network for the planned issue of every significant purchase order, then the purchase order value can be assigned to these activities. This makes possible the preparation of reports from the computer which will set the times for these costs when the orders are placed and thus give a schedule of purchase cost commitments.

If another activity is added for the receipt of goods against each of these purchase orders, the same order value can be assigned to these later activities. Using suitable computer techniques, cost schedules can be derived that relate to the time when invoices will become due. These schedules indicate cash flow requirements.

None of this would be possible with insufficient detail on the network. Figure 6.13 illustrates this case.

Should a large network be broken down into smaller networks?

Some companies like to draw outline networks of their projects, perhaps containing only 100 or 150 activities in fairly coarse detail. These are then used as higher level management controls, but they must be backed up later by more detailed networks produced for the various project departments or participants. All these smaller networks must be tied together in some way so that

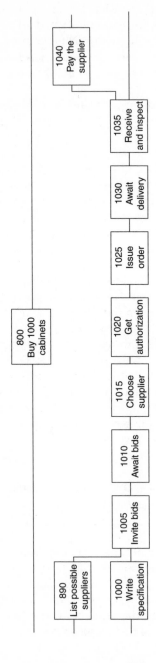

Figure 6.13 Level of detail in a purchasing sequence
Here are two possible extracts from a larger network, both concerned with the purchase of 1000 specially designed instrument cabinets for a new project. The total order value is about £100 000. The top diagram is one way to include this operation in the network, while the lower diagram goes to the opposite extreme and shows a considerable level of detail. The merits of choosing either of these options are discussed in the text.

their corresponding activities are scheduled on the same dates and have the same float.

This correlation can be achieved by designating all the detailed networks as subnetworks of the main control network and by identifying all activities shared between two or more networks as interface activities (see the following section).

Surprisingly large networks can be drawn on paper and followed through logically by hand and eye (although they must, for all practical purposes, ultimately be processed by a computer). I have worked successfully and without difficulty with networks that were initially drawn on long rolls of paper and contained well over a thousand activities. Large networks become more difficult to handle when they are not drawn on paper at all, but exist only in the computer. It is very difficult to trace the logic of a large network when only a few activities can be shown on the screen at a time, involving much scrolling in all directions. The best solution here is to use a plotter capable of taking either rolls or at least A0 sized sheets.

Interface activities

There are several circumstances in which an activity in one network can have a logical link with, or impose a constraint on, an activity in another network. The need to identify interface activities arises most frequently in projects where the total project network has been broken down into a number of smaller, more manageable subnetworks. This might be the result of a work breakdown or organizational breakdown decision.

There are occasions when a common interface appears in more than two subnetworks, for example when several subnetworks share the same start or finish.

Interfaces should only be allowed for true logical links. They should not be used in an attempt to depict operational problems such as competition for the use of a scarce resource (for which other methods will be described later).

Interfaces are highlighted on logic diagrams by giving the activity borders double ruled lines.

Milestones

Since the purpose of the network diagram is to produce a schedule from which project progress is to be initiated and controlled, intermediate points that can be used as benchmarks must be provided throughout the network and any resulting schedules. Activities that are considered to be particularly relevant are thus designated 'milestones'. A milestone is achieved when the relevant milestone activity is finished (in arrow networks, events can be designated as milestone events).

Computer programs for project scheduling allow reports to be filtered and printed so that they contain only such milestone activities, and these greatly help the assessment of progress against time and costs and are of value in reporting to higher management and to the customer.

Is the predicted timescale too long?

It is often found that the first forward pass through a network predicts a completion date that is unacceptably late. The planner will then be placed under great pressure to come up with an alternative plan to meet the required timescale (which might correspond to a delivery promise already made to a customer).

One option is to consider spending more money in additional resources, use of overtime or special machinery to speed up critical activities, a process sometimes called crashing. This, however, adds cost without adding value to the project and is to be avoided if at all possible. The planner might be tempted to cut estimates arbitrarily, perhaps on the advice of other managers, until the work fits neatly into the timescale. That must, of course, never be considered as a valid option unless good reasons can be given as to how the shorter times can be achieved.

A more sensible first course of action is to re-examine the network logic. Are all the constraints shown really constraints? Can any activities be overlapped, so that the start dates of some critical activities are brought forward? A process called 'fast-tracking' considers the performing of activities in parallel that have traditionally been performed serially, one after the other. In any case, a network should always be checked to ensure that it reflects the most practicable and efficient way of working.

Most networks use only simple start-finish relationships but the planner should always bear in mind the availability of complex notation (see Figure 6.7) and be prepared to use start-start or other complex links to overlap suitable activities and bring the planned completion date forward.

Early consideration of resource constraints

Nothing much has been said so far about possible scarcity of resources and the additional constraints that such problems might impose on the network logic or estimated activity durations.

Consider, for example, the most simple case of a resource constraint, where one particular individual is going to have to perform several network activities single-handed. Assume that this person cannot perform two activities at the same time. The planner, knowing this, might be tempted to add links to the network to indicate this constraint and prevent any two of these activities from being planned as simultaneous tasks. But if all these activities lie on different paths in a complex network where should the constraints be placed? Before time analysis has been done the planner cannot know in which order all these jobs should be performed.

Similar worries about resources might attach to other activities where the resource requirements are more complex, when several activities can be allowed to run in parallel or overlap provided that the total resources needed do not exceed the total available.

Fortunately there is a simple solution to the problem of all such resource constraints. At this stage in the planning, simply ignore them! The purpose of drawing the initial network is to establish the logic of the most desirable work pattern (assuming no resource constraints). Time analysis follows to establish the amount of float available, which effectively allots priority values to all activities. All this information provides a sound basis for subsequent resource scheduling, which is a quite separate procedure (described in the following chapter).

Planning and scheduling have to move forward one step at a time, and consideration of resource constraints is a step that is not taken when the first network is drawn. However, the planner must use common sense in this respect. Suppose that an activity requiring skilled fitters has been estimated to require 150 man-hours, and that several people could work on the task if required (without hindering each other to any serious extent). The duration for this activity would therefore depend on the number of people assigned:

- 1 fitter for 20 days
- 2 fitters for 10 days
- 3 fitters for 8 days
- 4 fitters for 7 days
  ... and so on.

The correct approach for the planner is to ask the manager (or delegate) of the department responsible to say how many fitters would be best for this task, and write the corresponding duration on the network. The possible demands of other activities on these fitters are disregarded at this stage. However, if the company only employs two suitable fitters in total, the planner would be stupid to schedule more than two for this or any other activity. This is where common sense comes in.

7

Scheduling

This chapter uses a small construction project to illustrate some of the principles of network time analysis and resource scheduling.

Resource scheduling

Resource scheduling is the process of converting a project plan into a working schedule that takes account of the resources which can be made available. The resulting schedule has to be practical, which means that undue peaks and troughs in workload should be smoothed out as far as possible, while still attempting to finish the project at the earliest or required time.

In those industries and professions where the bulk of work is contracted out to others, project planning will probably be adequate if taken only to the time analysis stage, with no need for resource scheduling. The task of resource scheduling must then be left to the subcontractors who employ the direct labour and other resources.

Most people will think of resource scheduling first in terms of people. But subjects for scheduling can include other resources such as plant and machinery, bulk materials and money. The treatment of these non-labour resources is generally similar to manpower scheduling, except that the names and units of quantity will change.

Resource scheduling is a complex subject and there are many possible methods. This chapter will concentrate on the simple, straightforward aspects. The essential principles will be explained during the course of the case study project.

The role of network analysis in resource scheduling

A network cannot normally be used by itself to demonstrate the volume of resources needed at any given point in project time. In fact, when the network is drawn no considered account can be taken of the resources which will be available. The start of each activity is usually assumed to be dependent only upon the completion of its preceding activities, and not on the availability of resources at the right time. This was explained at the end of the previous chapter.

The results of network time analysis are, however, used to determine activity priorities, which in turn decide how scarce resources should be allocated. Usually it is the activities with least remaining float that get the highest priority. Float is described in a separate section below, using data from the garage project that now follows.

Introducing the garage project

Project definition

A small firm of builders has been commissioned to erect a detached garage. The building is to be constructed of brick, with a concrete floor, corrugated sheet roof and roof lights instead of windows. The doors are to be made on site of timber and hung on strap hinges. No heavy lifting is involved in this project and no activity needs more than two people. The planned start date is 13 May 2002 and completion is required as soon as possible.

Resources available

The building firm engaged on the garage project is a small outfit, comprising the not unusual father and son team. The father, no longer capable of sustained heavy work, is nevertheless a good all-round craftsman with long experience. The son, on the other hand, can best be described as a strong, willing lad, sound in wind and limb but lacking any special experience or skill. This firm's resource availability can therefore be listed as follows:

Skilled persons	1 (stated as 1S for the computer)
Labourers	1 (stated as 1L for the computer)

If really stretched, this small company can call upon additional help, but it prefers to keep it in the family.

Task list and cost estimates

The task list for the garage project is shown in Figure 7.1. This lists all the principal tasks, together with their estimated materials costs. The activity ID codes refer to the network diagram, which is shown in Figure 7.2. The resource levels needed for each activity are written on the network diagram. For example, activity G1016 has a duration of two days and needs one skilled person and one labourer, as indicated by the codes 2d 1S 1L. This means, in practice, one skilled person and one labourer working full time for two days.

The task list in Figure 7.1 also gives the daily cost rates for these resources. So the estimated total cost for activity G1016 would be as follows:

1 skilled person for 2 days @ £160 per man-day	£320
1 labourer for 2 days @ £120 per man-day	£240
Materials	£60
Total estimated cost of activity G1016	£620

The total estimated cost of all materials and labour for the garage will not be known until the computer has scheduled the resources and calculated all the activity costs.

Activity ID	Activity description	Materials required	Materials cost (£)
START	Project start	No materials	
G0102	Dig foundations	No materials	
G0103	Make, prime door frame	Wood and primer	50
G0104	Dig soakaway, trench	No materials	
G0107	Make doors	Wood and sundries	300
G0110	Cut roof timbers	Wood	450
G0205	Concrete foundations	Concrete ingredients	150
G0305	Position door frame	No materials	
G0411	Lay underground pipe	Pipe	40
G0508	Build main brick walls	Bricks and mortar	650
G0509	Lay concrete base	Concrete ingredients	70
G0713	Prime the doors	Primer and sundries	20
G0810	Fit RSJ lintel	Rolled steel joist (RSJ)	40
G0913	Lay floor screed	Flooring compound	200
G1012	Fit roof timbers	No extra materials	
G1016	Case lintel, parapets	Wood and concrete	60
G1115	Fill drain trench	No materials	
G1214	Fit fascia boards	Wood	30
G1216	Fit roof sheets	Sheets and fixings	360
G1317	Hang doors	Locks and hinges	80
G1417	Fit gutters and pipes	Gutters, pipes, fixings	80
G1518	Concrete over trench	Concrete ingredients	20
G1618	Seal the roof	Sealant	30
G1718	Paint all woodwork	Paint and sundries	30
FINISH	Project finish	No materials	

Resource code	Resource name		Resource cost per day
S	Skilled worker		160
L	Labourer		120

Figure 7.1   Task list for the garage project

Project calendar

All scheduling will be based on a five-day working week. Saturdays and Sundays are therefore not counted as days available for work. In all the software used for this chapter this was the default

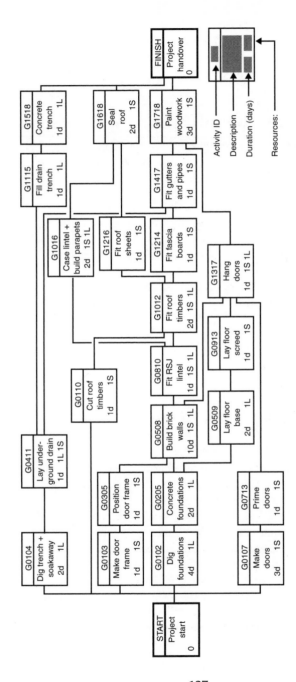

Figure 7.2 Garage project network diagram

127

calendar condition. Although public holidays would have inter-
vened in real life, they were ignored for this simple fictional case
study. All computer software will allow for public holidays to be
removed from the working calendar.

Garage project network planning

The network diagram

The network diagram in Figure 7.2 has deliberately been kept as
simple as possible for clarity. The plan assumes, for instance, that
all necessary materials and machinery will be on site when
needed. Also left out of this diagram is any provision for the time
needed for concrete to cure.

Remember that a network diagram takes no account of any possible constraints caused by two or more activities competing for
scarce resources. But, knowing that the firm only has one labourer
and one skilled person, no single activity has been estimated as
needing more than this father and son family workforce.

Initial time analysis

Figure 7.3 is the time analysis report produced by the computer.
In this instance I used Primavera. That is a high level, fairly
powerful program and, not surprisingly, it made short work of
this little project. The table shown in Figure 7.3 is part of a bigger
screen display which also includes a bar chart. Activities are listed
in ascending order of their early start dates.

Notice that the tabulation also gives the calculated cost for
every activity, which is the sum of labour and materials. When
these are added up, we discover that the garage is likely to cost a
total of £11 420. If the project starts as planned on 13 May 2002, it
should finish on 13 June 2002 provided that nothing goes terribly
wrong and that there are adequate resources. But a big question
mark hangs over those resources. Will the father and son team be
enough to carry out all this work in the time?

ID	Activity description	Dur	Early start	Early finish	Late start	Late finish	Total float	Free float	Budgeted cost
START	Project start	0	13MAY02		13MAY02		0	0	0.00
G0103	Make door frame	1	13MAY02	13MAY02	17MAY02	17MAY02	4	0	210.00
G0104	Dig trench and soakaway	2	13MAY02	14MAY02	05JUN02	06JUN02	17	0	240.00
G0102	Dig foundations	4	13MAY02	16MAY02	13MAY02	16MAY02	0	0	480.00
G0305	Position door frame	1	14MAY02	14MAY02	20MAY02	20MAY02	4	4	160.00
G0411	Lay underground drain	1	15MAY02	15MAY02	07JUN02	07JUN02	17	16	320.00
G0107	Make doors	3	15MAY02	17MAY02	04JUN02	06JUN02	14	0	780.00
G0205	Concrete foundations	2	17MAY02	20MAY02	17MAY02	20MAY02	0	0	390.00
G0110	Cut roof timbers	1	20MAY02	20MAY02	04JUN02	04JUN02	11	11	610.00
G0713	Prime doors	1	20MAY 02	20MAY02	07JUN02	07JUN02	14	10	180.00
G0509	Lay floor base	2	21MAY02	22MAY02	05JUN02	06JUN02	11	0	310.00
G0508	Build brick walls	10	21MAY02	03JUN02	21MAY02	03JUN02	0	0	3,450.00
G0913	Lay floor screed	1	23MAY02	23MAY02	07JUN02	07JUN02	11	7	360.00
G0810	Fit RSJ lintel	1	04JUN02	04JUN02	04JUN02	04JUN02	0	0	320.00
G1317	Hang doors	1	04JUN02	04JUN02	10JUN02	10JUN02	4	4	360.00
G1012	Fit roof timbers	2	05JUN02	06JUN02	05JUN02	06JUN02	0	0	560.00
G1016	Case lintel, build parapets	2	05JUN02	06JUN02	10JUN02	11JUN02	3	1	620.00
G1115	Fill drain trench	1	07JUN02	07JUN02	12JUN02	12JUN02	3	0	120.00
G1214	Fit fascia boards	1	07JUN02	07JUN02	07JUN02	07JUN02	0	0	190.00
G1216	Fit roof sheets	1	07JUN02	07JUN02	11JUN02	11JUN02	2	0	520.00
G1417	Fit gutters and pipes	1	10JUN02	10JUN02	10JUN02	10JUN02	0	0	240.00
G1518	Concrete drain trench	1	10JUN02	10JUN02	13JUN02	13JUN02	3	3	140.00
G1618	Seal roof	2	10JUN02	11JUN02	12JUN02	13JUN02	2	2	350.00
G1718	Paint all woodwork	3	11JUN02	13JUN02	11JUN02	13JUN02	0	0	510.00
FINISH	Project finish and handover	0		13JUN02		13JUN02	0	0	0.00

Figure 7.3 Time analysis for the garage project

129

A first look at the resource schedule

The bar chart in Figure 7.4 is simply a conversion of the time analysis data given in Figure 7.3. Each bar is coded to show the type of resource need, with solid black indicating one skilled person and the grey bars denoting the labourer.

All tasks have been placed at their earliest possible dates on the bar chart. A glance down some of the daily columns shows that there are days when more than one person of each grade will be needed, unless the various jobs can be rearranged. It is clear that some tasks must be deliberately delayed to smooth out work overloads. But how much can any task be delayed without affecting the project end date? That, of course, depends on how much float a task has.

Before going on to examine float in a little more detail, one assumption has to be made. The customer for this garage wants it built as soon as possible. Meanwhile her shiny new car is having to stand out in the street, unprotected night and day. So, if the garage could theoretically be finished on 13 June 2002, that's when the customer wants it.

All float calculations (the backward pass through the network) are therefore based on trying to achieve the earliest possible completion date of 13 June 2002.

Float

The network for the garage project (see Figure 7.2) and its time analysis will be used here to illustrate how float is classified and calculated. Project day numbers will be used because these are easier to use than calendar dates when analysing float.

Total float

Consider activity G0913, 'Lay floor screed'. For clarity, this activity is shown as a separate detail in Figure 7.5, which also includes a tiny but highly relevant fragment of the project bar chart. A glance at the network fragment shows that the earliest possible start for this activity is day 8 (which means the end of day 8). The

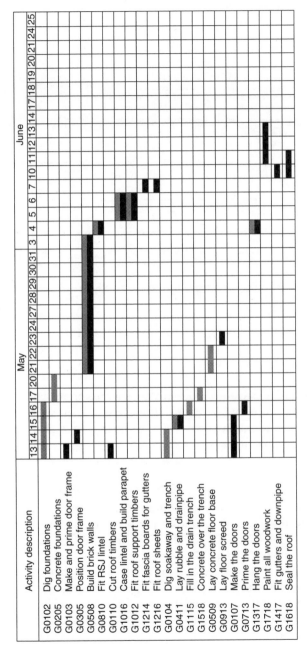

Figure 7.4 Bar chart for the garage project

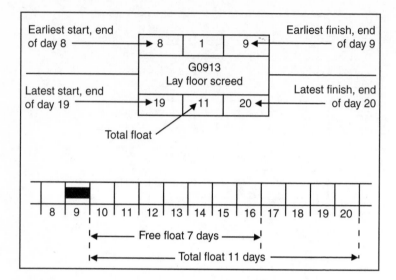

Figure 7.5   Float analysis of a garage project activity

latest permissible finish is the end of day 20. Allowing for the one day's duration of this activity, it is easy to see that its start (and finish) could be delayed by up to 11 days without causing delay to the activities that follow. This 11 days is the total float possessed by the activity.

Total float is defined as the amount by which an activity can be delayed if all its preceding activities take place at their earliest possible times and following activities are allowed to wait until their latest permissible times.

Free float

If, because of delays in the project or through intentional resource scheduling, the floor screed operation takes place later than its earliest possible time, some (if not all) of its float will be eroded. This will usually have a 'knock-on' effect through the network, robbing some of the float from activities which follow because they can no longer be started at their earliest possible times. In fact the float for any activity must always be seen in relation to how it might affect, or be affected by, the float possessed by other activities in the network.

Consideration of these effects gives rise to definitions for two types of float in addition to total float. These are free float (described here) and independent float (see below).

Free float is the amount of float available for an activity when all its preceding activities actually take place at their earliest possible times and following activities can still take place at their earliest possible times. This condition can only arise when an activity has more than one logical link at each end, and most activities will have zero free float.

However, the computer has calculated that activity G0913 has seven days' free float (see Figure 7.5). This can be verified by mental analysis of the network, which is easier to do when arrow notation is used.

Independent float

Independent float is quite rare and can only arise when the network logic allows an activity float that is truly independent of its predecessors and successors.

Independent float is the amount of float available for an activity when all succeeding activities can take place at their earliest possible times even though the preceding activities have been delayed up to their latest permissible times.

In fact, for those readers who are interested, activity G1016, 'Case lintel and build parapets', does have independent float. It is really necessary to view this on an arrow diagram rather than the precedence network used here. The complete float analysis for activity G1016 is as follows:

Total float	3 days
Free float	1 day
Independent float	1 day

The explanation for this, backed up by an arrow diagram, is given in Lock (2000).

Remaining float

The total float possessed by any activity is at risk of erosion from the moment that project resource scheduling starts right up to the time when the activity is completed. Total float can be reduced, for example, as a result of a conscious decision to delay the planned start of an activity as part of the resource scheduling process (in order to plan a smoother workload pattern). There is also the obvious risk that preceding activities will run late, absorbing some or all of the total float.

For practical purposes, once a project is started the project manager is not interested in the total float that an activity had in the beginning, when the network was first drawn. It is the residue of the total float still possessed by each uncompleted activity that should concern the project manager. This is the remaining float.

Activities with negative float

Suppose that the critical path through a network has a total estimated duration of 100 weeks. The end activity will therefore have an earliest possible completion time of 100. Barring other considerations, the latest permissible completion time for the project will also be at the end of the 100th week. Time analysis will, in the usual way, produce one or more critical paths back through to the start of the network in which all the critical activities have zero total float.

Suppose, however, that those 'other considerations' include a promise to the customer that the project will be completed in 90 weeks. The latest permissible project end date is therefore 10 weeks before its earliest possible date. All activities that were previously on the critical path with zero total float will now have a total float of minus 10 weeks.

Negative float can be caused whenever scheduled target dates are imposed on the end activity, or indeed on any other activity in a project network. Negative float occurs in the schedule shown in Figure 7.9, caused by resource limitations that will be explained later.

Garage project resource scheduling

For the examples in this chapter resource scheduling has been carried out both mentally and using a computer. The mental solutions were only possible because of the very small size of this project.

Before project managers had access to computers, all scheduling had to be done manually and the most convenient method was based on the use of charting boards. Bar charts could be set up in such a way that the tasks could be moved backwards and forwards until a smooth workload was achieved. Of course, observing all the dependencies between activities was quite an art and sometimes very tedious.

The histograms in Figure 7.6 were calculated by hand and repeated, somewhat less perfectly, using a number of different computer programs. For the present purpose it does not matter how the charts were produced: they are presented here to demonstrate the basic concepts of resource scheduling (or, as many describe it, resource levelling).

Resource aggregation

Look first at the top pair of histograms in Figure 7.6. These show the numbers of each resource type that would be needed on each weekday to perform all the garage project activities on their earliest possible dates, as shown in Figure 7.3. The bar chart in Figure 7.4 can be used to arrive at these results, simply by totalling the number of black and grey bars in each daily column.

If resources were available in ample supply, then perhaps this schedule could be accepted. However, we know that the garage team has only one skilled and one unskilled person available. Also, any schedule that has peak workloads interspersed with idle periods is inefficient and inconvenient.

Resource-limited schedule

Suppose now that the garage builder has decided that on no account will he hire any help, so the work must all be done by himself and his son.

A plan to satisfy this requirement, known as a resource-limited schedule, can be calculated either by using a computer or, for such a small project, by using an adjustable bar chart. Whichever method is used, the process is the same. Activities are moved to later dates if no resources are available. Activities with float are

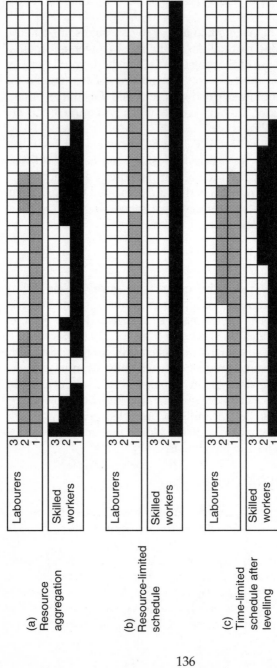

Figure 7.6 Resource histograms for the garage project

136

moved first but, if absolutely necessary, some critical activities might have to be moved and the project end date will be delayed. The result for the garage project is shown in Figure 7.6 at (b). The very smooth, optimized result shown here was calculated mentally. I also ran this calculation using several different computer programs and they generally produced the same result. The end date has been put back from 13 June to 26 June 2002.

One of the programs which I used for this calculation was the old MS-DOS version of Open Plan. I also ran that schedule using the current Open Plan Professional version but I particularly like the screen commentary that appears using the older version. The result, for the resource-limited run, is shown in Figure 7.7. The tabulation warns that the named activities have had to be delayed owing to lack of available resources.

Figure 7.9 (see page 142) displays data produced by Primavera for the resource-limited run. This shows that the earliest possible dates are, in many cases, later than the latest permissible dates because of the resource-limited scheduling. Negative float has been generated as a result.

Time-limited resource levelling for the garage project

Unfortunately for the master builder of the garage project, the customer is vociferous. Her raised voice has attracted quite a

```
Open Plan (R)  PDM Resource Scheduling     Project: GARAGE
Revision 5.10                              Resource Limited Schedule.
                                           Out-of-sequence process option O.
Copyright (c) 1985-1994, WST Corp.         Smoothing Option is ON.
                                           Hard Zero option is ON.
Company: DENNIS LOCK                        Finish date is 27JUN02 .
Serial:        64 AQAS

Start Time: 16:55:27

Delaying activity G0509 due to resource LA.
Delaying activity G0110 due to resource SK.
Delaying activity G1012 due to resource LA.
Delaying activity G1216 due to resource SK.
Delaying activity G0107 due to resource SK.
Delaying activity G0713 due to resource SK.
Delaying activity G1317 due to resource LA.
Delaying activity G0104 due to resource LA.
Delaying activity G0411 due to resource SK.

Normal end of job.  Send error log to (P) rinter  (d) isk or <SPACE> to skip?
Elapsed time    :00:02         (100% complete)
```

Figure 7.7 Resource scheduling error log, garage project, resource-limited

doorstep audience and she has left the builder and everyone else within earshot in no doubt that she will not wait until 26 June for her garage. She insists on having her car safely under cover by the evening of 13 June. The schedule must, therefore, be recalculated.

In this case, the answer is to plan to complete the garage by its earliest possible time analysis date, take on additional resources as required, but adjust the timings of individual activities within their float to remove the workload peaks as far as possible. The earliest dates shown in Figure 7.3 must stand for critical tasks.

The histograms at (c) in Figure 7.6 resulted from rescheduling the garage project manually. Now the project can still be completed by 13 June. It is true that extra resources are needed, but these are fewer and better planned than the result obtained from simple aggregation.

Extra resource availability can sometimes be provided simply by asking the existing people to work longer hours. However, projects should not be scheduled with the intention of using overtime. As work on the project proceeds, overtime can become a valuable reserve resource, to be called upon in emergencies, when critical activities are in danger of running late. Overtime should normally be held in reserve against such contingencies, and the stated resource availability levels should be limited to the capacities present during normal working hours.

The error report shown in Figure 7.8 appeared on screen when I ran the garage project as a time-limited schedule using the MS-DOS version of Open Plan. This shows clearly the actions taken by the program to avoid unnecessary peaks and attempt a smooth work pattern.

Computer reports for the garage project

Proprietary project management software usually contains a wide range of inbuilt report formats that can be used 'off the shelf'. Several examples have already been presented in this chapter.

Many programs give the project manager the option of creating new report formats to suit his or her own project needs.

Plotters can be arranged to print network diagrams, bar chart conversions and all manner of other graphical displays, enhanced

```
Open Plan (R) PDM Resource Scheduling      Project: GARAGE
Revision 5.10                              Resource Limited (leveled) Schedule.
Copyright (c) 1985–1994, WST Corp.         Out-of-sequence process option O.
                                           Smoothing Option is ON.
Company: DENNIS LOCK                        Finish date is 13JUN02 .
Serial:        64 AQAS
Start Time: 21:00:11

Activity    G1216 exceeds resource SK by          1.
Delaying activity G1016 due to resource LA.
Activity    G0509 exceeds resource LA by          1.
Delaying activity G0107 due to resource SK.
Delaying activity G1317 due to resource LA.
Activity    G1317 exceeds resource SK by          2.
Delaying activity G1115 due to resource LA.


Normal end of job.  Send error log to (P) rinter   (d) isk or <SPACE> to skip?
Elapsed time        :00:03          (100% complete)
```

Figure 7.8   Resource scheduling error log, garage project, time-limited

by the use of colour. Cost control data can be linked to the schedules, allowing budget cost curves, cost tables and other presentations of planned and recorded expenditure to be printed. All data can usually be interchanged with other IT systems or transmitted over the Internet.

Network plots

A network plot is useful at an early stage in the data processing proceedings. This greatly assists in checking through the logic to make sure that every link and activity has been put in the right place during data entry.

Computer programs vary considerably in their ability to plot networks sensibly. One very popular program is particularly weak in this respect, typically showing links going from right to left, with many avoidable crossovers and ambiguities. Primavera and Open Plan Professional both performed well when asked to plot the garage project.

Unfortunately, all network plots tend to spread over large areas of paper. A planner whose printer can only accept A4 sheets will find that, for any network, the plot is likely to take up many sheets which all have to be cut and pasted together before a complete network can be seen. For this reason, I have chosen not to attempt illustrating the results on the small pages of this book.

Filtering

After a big network has been processed, a large volume of data is stored in the computer. Computers are capable of producing output reports in many different forms, even from a small amount of data. If all possible reports were to be produced, the result might be an unmanageable pile of paper, impressive for its bulk, but not for much else. It follows that the project manager must manage the data carefully, ensuring that reports are concise, well presented and as effective as possible for their intended purpose.

The data content of every report must be carefully considered, so that each recipient gets information that is particularly useful or relevant to him or her (preferably on a 'need-to-know' basis). This is achieved by the process of filtering (editing), made possible by the provision of departmental report codes for all activity records, or by specifying milestones or key activities, by reporting on selected resources or by choosing other activity characteristics. Most programs provide a menu from which filtering options can be selected.

All unwanted data should be excluded from reports. For example, the planner might choose to filter out all activities that have already been completed.

Sorting

Another important aspect of reports is the sequence in which data are presented. This is achieved by the process of sorting.

For example, a departmental manager or supervisor responsible for issuing work needs a report which lists jobs in order of their earliest or scheduled start dates. A progress clerk or expediter is best served by a report that lists jobs or materials deliveries in order of their completion dates.

Work-to lists

A tabulation of all activities sorted in order of their scheduled start dates is the prime tool for issuing work. If such reports can be produced after resource levelling and then filtered to suit each manager on the project, every recipient of the report can feel confident because of the following:

- Every job has been sequenced logically by network analysis so that it should not be scheduled to start before it is feasible technically.

- The rate of working expected from each department or, in other words, the number of activities shown as starting in each period, should be possible to perform with the available resources.

For these reasons, activity lists produced after resource scheduling are sometimes called 'work-to lists'. Figure 7.9 is the resource-limited work-to list for the garage project produced by Primavera. The columns headed 'Early start' and 'Early finish' give the recommended (scheduled) working dates. The 'latest' dates are for information only, being the latest dates needed to finish the project by 13 June, now impossible owing to the limited resources.

Resource and cost tables

If the system has been used for resource scheduling it should be capable of printing tables of expected resource usage. When cost rates have been specified for resources, cost data can also be included in the reports, and this information will automatically be timed according to the plan. Such reports can be produced for each type of resource, for each department or for all activities in the project.

Figure 7.10 is a screen view of a cost report for the garage project produced by Primavera. The timing in this version is for the resource-limited schedule. Each vertical bar is proportional to the estimated daily cost of the project, so the computer has produced a kind of cash flow schedule. The graph shows the cumulative expenditure, which is seen to reach the project total of £11 420 at the extreme right-hand edge of the chart.

Tabulations are usually to be preferred to graphs because they remove the need for scaling, with all the reading errors and inaccuracies that must follow. All programs are capable of producing tabulations in various forms. Microsoft Project can display data in

ID	Activity description	Dur	Early start	Early finish	Late start	Late finish	Total float	Free float	Budgeted cost
START	Project start	0	13MAY02		13MAY02		0	0	0.00
G0103	Make door frame	1	13MAY02	13MAY02	17MAY02	17MAY02	4	0	210.00
G0102	Dig foundations	4	13MAY02	16MAY02	13MAY02	16MAY02	0	0	480.00
G0305	Position door frame	1	14MAY02	14MAY02	20MAY02	20MAY02	4	4	160.00
G0107	Make doors	3	15MAY02	17MAY02	04JUN02	06JUN02	14	15	780.00
G0205	Concrete foundations	2	17MAY02	20MAY02	17MAY02	20MAY02	0	0	390.00
G0110	Cut roof timbers	1	20MAY02	20MAY02	04JUN02	04JUN02	11	11	610.00
G0508	Build brick walls	10	21MAY02	03JUN02	21MAY02	03JUN02	0	0	3,450.00
G0810	Fit RSJ lintel	1	04JUN02	04JUN02	04JUN02	04JUN02	0	0	320.00
G1012	Fit roof timbers	2	05JUN02	06JUN02	05JUN02	06JUN02	0	0	560.00
G1214	Fit fascia boards	1	07JUN02	07JUN02	07JUN02	07JUN02	0	4	190.00
G0509	Lay floor base	2	07JUN02	10JUN02	05JUN02	06JUN02	-2	0	310.00
G0713	Prime doors	1	10JUN02	10JUN02	07JUN02	07JUN02	-1	6	180.00
G0913	Lay floor screed	1	11JUN02	11JUN02	07JUN02	07JUN02	-2	5	360.00
G0104	Dig trench and soakaway	2	11JUN02	12JUN02	05JUN02	06JUN02	-4	0	240.00
G1216	Fit roof sheets	1	12JUN02	12JUN02	11JUN02	11JUN02	-1	8	520.00
G0411	Lay underground drain	1	13JUN02	13JUN02	07JUN02	07JUN02	-4	0	320.00
G1115	Fill drain trench	1	14JUN02	14JUN02	12JUN02	12JUN02	-2	3	120.00
G1417	Fit gutters and pipes	1	14JUN02	14JUN02	10JUN02	10JUN02	-4	3	240.00
G1016	Case lintel, build parapets	2	17JUN02	18JUN02	10JUN02	11JUN02	-5	4	620.00
G1317	Hang doors	1	19JUN02	19JUN02	10JUN02	10JUN02	-7	0	360.00
G1518	Concrete drain trench	1	20JUN02	20JUN02	13JUN02	13JUN02	-5	4	140.00
G0718	Paint all woodwork	3	20JUN02	24JUN02	11JUN02	13JUN02	-7	2	510.00
G1618	Seal roof	2	25JUN02	26JUN02	12JUN02	13JUN02	-9	0	350.00
FINISH	Project finish and handover	0	26JUN02		13JUN02		-9	0	0.00

Figure 7.9 Resource-limited work-to list for the garage project

142

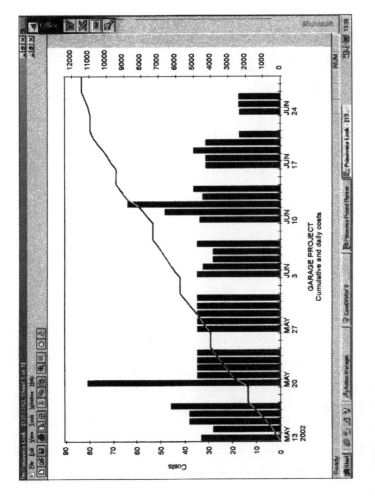

Figure 7.10 Cost/time graphs for the garage project

143

144 The Essentials of Project Management

reports somewhat similar to the table in Figure 7.11, for example, although my example has been restructured and partly simulated for greater clarity in this book. The costs have been set out on a day-by-day basis, with expenditure shown to stop on the resource-limited completion date of 27 June. The estimated total project cost is seen to reach £11 420 in the right-hand column.

Executive summary reports

Most programs make provision for one-page project summary reports, intended as a management overview. If more than one project is contained in the system, some programs will allow summary reports to be printed out concisely for all these projects in a type of report sometimes known as a project directory.

Conclusions

Modern project management software offers many powerful features, only a very small sample of which could be discussed here. Among features not mentioned here are the various forms of risk analysis and prediction. The greatest benefits in terms of improved cost and progress performance are seen when an organization can successfully implement network-based resource scheduling across its entire workload. That is a process called multiproject scheduling or, sometimes, programme management. An insight into these possibilities and computer applications in general is given in Lock (2000).

Reference

Lock, D. (2000), *Project Management*, 7th edn, Aldershot, Gower.

GARAGE PROJECT SCHEDULED RESOURCE USAGE AND COST										
	Resource LA: Labourer				Resource SK: Skilled				Task matls (£)	Cum. cost (£)
Date	Avail.	Used	Not used	Cost (£)	Avail.	Used	Not used	Cost (£)		
13 May 02	1	1		120	1	1		160	50	330
14 May 02	1	1		120	1	1		160		610
15 May 02	1	1		120	1	1		160	100	990
16 May 02	1	1		120	1	1		160	100	1,370
17 May 02	1	1		120	1	1		160	175	1,825
20 May 02	1	1		120	1	1		160	525	2,630
21 May 02	1	1		120	1	1		160	65	2,975
22 May 02	1	1		120	1	1		160	65	3,320
23 May 02	1	1		120	1	1		160	65	3,665
24 May 02	1	1		120	1	1		160	65	4,010
27 May 02	1	1		120	1	1		160	65	4,355
28 May 02	1	1		120	1	1		160	65	4,700
29 May 02	1	1		120	1	1		160	65	5,045
30 May 02	1	1		120	1	1		160	65	5,390
31 May 02	1	1		120	1	1		160	65	5,735
03 Jun 02	1	1		120	1	1		160	65	6,080
04 Jun 02	1	1		120	1	1		160	40	6,400
05 Jun 02	1	1		120	1	1		160		6,680
06 Jun 02	1	1		120	1	1		160		6,960
07 Jun 02	1	1		120	1	1		160	65	7,305
10 Jun 02	1	1		120	1	1		160	55	7,640
12 Jun 02	1	1		120	1	1		160	200	8,120
13 Jun 02	1	1		120	1	1		160	360	8,760
14 Jun 02	1	1		120	1	1		160	40	9,080
17 Jun 02	1	1		120	1	1		160	80	9,440
18 Jun 02	1	1		120	1	1		160	30	9,750
19 Jun 02	1	1		120	1	1		160	30	10,060
20 Jun 02	1	1		120	1	1		160	80	10,420
21 Jun 02	1	1		120	1	1		160	30	10,730
24 Jun 02	1		1		1	1		160	10	10,900
25 Jun 02	1		1		1	1		160	10	11,070
26 Jun 02	1		1		1	1		160	15	11,245
27 Jun 02	1		1		1	1		160	15	11,420
28 Jun 02	1		1		1		1			11,420
01 Jul 02	1		1		1		1			11,420
02 Jul 02	1		1		1		1			11,420
03 Jul 02	1		1		1		1			11,420
04 Jul 02	1		1		1		1			11,420
05 Jul 02	1		1		1		1			11,420
	1		1		1		1			11,420

Figure 7.11   A useful resource and cost tabulation for the garage project

8

Implementation

Once authorization has been received, the project ceases to be merely an object for planning and speculation and becomes instead a live entity, to which the contractor is fully committed. For the purposes of achieving all the project objectives, whether technical, budgetary or timescale, the appropriate project organization has to be set up. All participants must be made fully aware of the particular role they will be expected to play. A common risk to projects is failure to start work on time. Very long delays can be caused by prevarication, legal or planning difficulties, shortage of information, lack of funds or other resources and a host of other reasons. All of these factors can place a project manager in a difficult or impossible position. If a project is not allowed to start on time it can hardly be expected to finish on time.

Project authorization

In the context of this chapter, authorization by the customer or project owner means that the contractor has been given formal written instruction to proceed with the project on terms that have previously been negotiated and agreed. For in-house projects, the 'customer' is the company itself and the contractor is the responsible division or department within the organization.

Initial registration and numbering

Once a new project has entered an organization, it has to be formally 'entered into the system' so that all the necessary accounting, planning, progressing and other administrative procedures can be put in place.

One of the very first steps is to add the new project to the project register and allocate a project number. This number should preferably be built in as an identifier to drawing and equipment specification numbers, cost codes, time sheets and all other important project documentation.

Whenever it is necessary to retrieve information about a project, current or long past, the project register or its archived information is usually the best, even the only, starting place. In most management information systems or archives, the project number is the essential element leading to the various document files and project data. However, a well-kept register should allow any project and its former manager's name to be traced from the customer's name, project description, approximate date or other information long after the project number has been forgotten.

Internal project authorization document

The first step towards project implementation in any well-run company is the issue of an authorization document. Entitled 'project authorization' or perhaps 'works order', this document should define the departmental and purchasing cost budgets and give planned start and finish dates, details of the customer's order, pricing information, invoicing and delivery instructions and so on. One necessary item on a project authorization is the signature of a member of the contractor's senior management. This is the signal that the project is properly authorized and that work can begin.

An example of a project authorization form is given in Figure 8.1. This comes from a mining engineering company and has more detailed budget information on its reverse side.

PROJECT AUTHORIZATION

Client _____

Scope of work _____

_____

_____

_____

_____

Source documents _____

_____

Project number (to be entered by accounts department)

Project title (for computer reports)

Project manager (name) _____ Staff number

Project engineer (name) _____ Staff number

Project start date (enter as 01-JAN-03)

Target finish date (enter as 01-JAN-03)

Contract type:
Reimbursable ☐   Lump sum ☐   Other (Specify) _____

Estimate of man-hours

Standard cost grade	1	2	3	4	5	6	7	8
Man-hour totals								

Notes:

···   ··
Authorization (1)   *Authorization (2)*

Project manager		Marketing		Contracts dept.		Purchasing		
Project eng.		Central registry		Cost/planning		Accounts dept.		

Figure 8.1   Project authorization form

Project authorizations are usually distributed to all company departments for general information, but the supporting technical and commercial documents are only handed over to the project manager. It becomes the project manager's responsibility thereafter to ensure that all other managers in the organization are made aware of project requirements in detail, and sufficiently in advance to enable them to make any necessary preparations.

Preliminary organization of the project

Even when a clear technical specification has been prepared there are often many loose ends to be tied up before actual work can start. The extent and nature of these preliminary activities naturally depend on the type and size of project.

Charting the organization

When the project manager has been named, an organization chart (sometimes, unfortunately, called an organigram) should be drawn up and published to show all key people or agencies concerned with the project. It must include senior members of all external groups who are to have any responsibility in the project. If the organization is very large, the usual arrangement is to produce a summary chart and then draw a series of smaller charts which allow some of the groups to be shown in more detail. Depending, of course, on the actual arrangements, a comprehensive project organization chart might have to show the following information:

1 Key elements in the contractor's own organization, obviously including the project manager.
2 Management teams working away from the contractor's head office (especially site teams on construction projects).
3 Principal subcontractors.
4 External purchasing agent (if employed) together with any outside groups responsible for expediting, equipment inspection and shipping arrangements.
5 Independent consultants, acting for the customer, the contractor or third party (such as a finance house).

6 Representatives of government or local government departments (if relevant).

Responsibility matrix

People must know what is expected of them. One tool which can assist the project manager to allocate responsibilities is the responsibility matrix, an example of which is shown in Figure 8.2. The job titles of key members of the organization are listed above the matrix columns and various important task types are listed along the rows. Symbols are placed at the appropriate matrix intersec-

Task type	The client	Project manager	Project engineer	Purchasing mngr	Drawing office	Construction mngr	Planning engineer	Cost engineer	Project accountant
Make designs			+		●				
Approve designs	●	■	+						
Purchase enquiries		■	+	●					
Purchase orders	■	■	+	●					
Planning	■	■	+	+	+	+	●	+	
Cost control		●	+			+		+	
Progress reports		●	+	+	+	+			
Cost reports		●	+			+		+	+

Key

● Principal responsibility (only one per task)

+ Secondary responsibility

■ Must be consulted

Figure 8.2 A responsibility matrix

tions to show primary and secondary responsibility for each of the task types listed.

The responsibility matrix is best suited to deal with task categories rather than listing all the detailed tasks themselves. For example, it can show the person responsible for approving new designs in general, but it is not the place in which to list all the drawings that carry those designs.

Correspondence and document distribution

The contractor will be well advised to take control procedures for project correspondence seriously. The contractor could easily find itself in a difficult position if it were to lose vital letters or other documents. Thus positive steps must be taken to deal with the routeing and control of documented information within the home office and with all external parts of the project organization.

Nominated addressees or contacts

It is good practice for each organization to nominate one of its senior members to act as a control point for receiving and sending all formal written communications and technical documents, whether these are transmitted by mail, e-mail, airfreight, courier, facsimile or telex. Each nominated addressee then becomes responsible for seeing that the documents or the information contained in them is made known to all relevant people within their own organization.

Deciding document distribution

Most projects generate many documents. Once the planning, control and administrative procedures have been decided, all the associated forms, expected reports and other types of documents can be listed. It is then possible to consider each of these document types in turn and decide who needs to receive copies as a matter of routine. This should usually be on a 'need-to-know' rather than 'want-to-know' basis (except that all requests for documents from the customer must obviously be looked upon favourably unless these would give away information that the contractor wishes to remain confidential).

If the documents are to be made available in electronic form, accessible over a network, it might be necessary to impose different levels of access for security purposes, thus preventing unauthorized people from seeing sensitive or confidential data.

Once the regular distribution or availability of documents has been agreed, the decision can be depicted on a chart arranged as a matrix (which is, of course, secondary to the responsibility matrix shown in Figure 8.2). The names of the authorized recipients can be listed at the column heads, with the document names or types listed down the left-hand side. A tick in the square at each grid intersection shows that access is permissible. Alternatively, a number written at the intersection shows how many hard copies of the relevant document each person should receive. Letter codes can also be introduced if desired, so that 'O', for example, might indicate an original document, 'P' a paper print, 'S' a submaster or reproducible print of a drawing and 'M' a microfilm record. Figure 8.3 illustrates the principle.

DOCUMENTS	Customer	General manager	Project manager	Project engineer	Works manager	Production control	Buyer	Quality manager	HRM manager	Accountant	etc.
Bought-out parts lists				1		1	2	1			
Materials specifications				1			1	1			
Purchase requisitions							1				
Purchase orders							1			1	
Shortage lists			1			1	1				
Committed cost reports		1	1	1			1			1	
Drawing list				1	1						
Drawings for approval	1			1							
Approved drawings				1			1	1			
Network diagrams			1	1	1						
Summary manpower plans		1	1						1		
Summary bar charts		1	1								
Monthly reports	1	1	1				1				

RECIPIENTS

Extend as necessary →

etc.

Figure 8.3   A document distribution matrix

Project design standards and procedures

The contractor will have to investigate whether or not the project calls for any special design standards, safety requirements or compliance with government or other statutory regulations. These issues usually have cost implications and it is to be hoped that most of the requirements will have been established at the project definition stage.

It is often agreed that the drawings made for a project are the property of the customer, which will expect to take possession of all the original drawings at the end of the project and file them in its own system (the contractor would, of course, retain a complete copy).

The contractor might be asked to use the customer's own system for drawing numbers. Common practice in such cases is to number each drawing twice, using the customer's system and the contractor's normal standard. These dual numbers can be cross-referenced in the computer or, failing that, the drawing register.

The drawings might have to be made on the customer's own standard drawing sheet format, in which case the contractor must obtain either supplies or the sheet design data as soon as possible.

Choice of planning and control procedures

Companies accustomed to carrying out large projects may have at their disposal a considerable range of planning and control procedures. At the start of each new project these can be reviewed to determine which should be used. Factors affecting this choice are the size and complexity of the project, the degree of difficulty and risk expected in meeting the end objectives, the number and locations of outside organizations and the wishes or directions of the customer.

Procedures manual

For some projects contractors will compile a procedures manual. This will list the particular procedures that will apply to the project and include such things as the names of key personnel, organization charts, responsibility matrix, document distribution matrix and the names and addresses of all key organizations with their relevant incoming and outgoing correspondence prefix codes.

Physical preparations and organization

Physical preparations must be made for any project that requires accommodation, plant, equipment, services such as gas, electric power, compressed air, water and so on. There is no typical case, because the requirements of every project depend very much on the nature of the project and the practices of its contractor. At one end of the scale is the project which will simply follow another in a factory, using the same staff, management and facilities. At the opposite extreme is the international project involving several large companies and a construction site in the middle of a desert with no communicating rail or road and no other infrastructure. In the latter case, making physical preparation for the main project is, in itself, a collection of very large subprojects.

Any discussion in this chapter must, therefore, be in general terms. None the less one or two important, general principles can be mentioned.

Importance of checklists

All project managers will know the frustration caused during the initial days and weeks when, keen to start and with deadlines to meet, real work has to wait because there is no information, no staff and a general lack of other facilities. Lack of information is often the worst of these problems: not necessarily about the main objectives and features of the intended project but more likely about a hundred and one annoying details which have to be resolved before work can start.

The value of checklists is mentioned in several places in this book, and no apology is needed or made for giving additional space to this subject here. Standard checklists, applicable to all projects, present and future, can be used as questionnaires to pre-empt information requirements. The best checklists are developed and refined gradually through experience, so that lessons learned on one project are remembered, added to those already learned and then put to use on projects which follow.

Construction site example

An instance where a checklist is particularly useful is when a construction site organization has to be established, especially when this is to be overseas. Even for an experienced organization, that can be an enormous operation. All sorts of questions have to be asked, and answered. Some questions should already have been answered when the proposal was researched (see Figure 2.2, page 16, for example). When the project becomes real, the questions and answers are of a more definite and detailed nature:

- How many people are going to be needed on site?
- How many of these will be:

    - our own permanent staff, on overseas assignment?
    - our own fixed term contract staff, hired for the purpose and duration only?
    - local recruits (will they need training?)?
    - client's staff?
    - subcontractors and their staff?

- What accommodation will be required?

    - how much?
    - what standard?
    - who is responsible for providing it?
    - rent free?

- What are the immigration rules?

    - passports and visas?
    - work permits?
    - any racial prejudices?

- Local employment laws and practices?
- What about expatriates' wives and families?
- Standard terms of employment?
- Pay and taxation arrangements?
- Insurances:

- – staff related?
- – work related?

● Staff medical, welfare and leisure facilities?
● Climate?
● Site access:

- – road?
- – rail?
- – air?
- – other?

● Vehicle fleet:

- – personnel carriers?
- – goods?
- – how provided?
- – how managed and maintained?

● Site plan:

- – what is needed?
- – when?
- – how provided?
- – how maintained?

… and so on for page after page, covering all aspects of the site and its legal, political and physical environment.

These questions need to be answered as completely and as early as possible. The better the checklist, the earlier and more completely the information will be obtained.

Getting work started

The kick-off meeting

When the newly appointed project manager has collected his or her wits and absorbed the contents of the project specification (which will probably entail some candle-burning), the most urgent job is to mobilize all the project resources and tell the key participants what is expected of them.

This process takes place in different stages and by a variety of methods. The first executive action of the project manager is usually to call an initial meeting, often called the 'kick-off' meeting, which gives the project manager the opportunity to outline the main features of the project to managers whose departments will work on the project, and to the most senior design staff and other key people.

If the project is organized as a team, the project manager will have the advantage of talking to people who are directly responsible to him or her. If the organization is a functional matrix, the task is more difficult – even getting people to attend the meeting becomes more a question of invitation or persuasion than a direct summons.

Whatever the circumstances, the skilled project manager will make the best possible use of the initial meeting to get the project off to a good start. Everyone who attends the meeting should leave with a clear picture of the project's objectives, the part that they are expected to play in achieving them and a sense of keenness and motivation to get on with the job.

Issuing initial planning information

It must be assumed that some degree of work planning has been carried out, either in advance or immediately following authorization. The resulting plans and schedules will do no good at all if they are merely regarded thereafter as objects to be gazed at and admired. The project manager must make certain that the contents of these schedules are made known to every key person in the organization.

At this stage, the plans will probably not exist in sufficient detail for issuing and controlling work on mainstream activities, but two aspects of planning at this initial stage have to be mentioned:

1   Even though the first bar chart or outline network planning might have been made in very coarse detail, and with vital gaps in knowledge of how the project is going to be conducted, those early plans will probably have been used in the project proposal. When authorization is received, the time framework for the project will already have been promised or declared to the project purchaser.

2 Although no detailed plans exist, none should be required right at the start, when the main task is to resolve questions of administration, set-up procedures and design concept finalization.

Two sets of initial plans should, therefore, be available for issue right at the start. The first of these is the summary plan giving committed dates for the whole project. This should accompany the works order or other project authorization document. It might be a bar chart. It can, for this purpose, simply be a tabulation of the key dates.

The other issue is the checklist and plan for preliminary activities, which the project manager will need to get the project started in a logical, systematic and efficient way.

One urgent job during the early period covered by the checklist must, of course, be to make the detailed plans and working schedules for the project (usually worked and reworked until they satisfy the delivery commitments already made in the project proposal).

Checklist and plan for preliminary activities

Every contractor develops its own expertise, according to the particular industry in which it operates. The contractor learns the sort of preliminary activities which must be carried out to establish procedures and design standards before a typical project can start. A sensible contractor will write these into a standard checklist. One company in my experience designed such a checklist in the form of a standard network diagram, a copy of which was used at the start of each new project. Time estimates and time analysis were never used on this standard network. It was used only as a checklist, but its value lay in the fact that it listed all potential preliminary activities in their logical sequence.

Detailed planning and work instructions

Importance of personal agreement and commitment

Enough has already been written in earlier chapters about the methods available for producing plans and working schedules. If the project is of any significance at all in terms of its size, complexity or perceived importance, it must be taken for granted that detailed planning will be performed, and that this will involve at least one senior representative from every key project function.

Each key participant must, therefore, have some share in formulating and agreeing the detailed plan. This is just as it should be, because no plan can be imposed successfully in isolation. It must carry the acceptance and support of those who are to be bound by it.

As soon as detailed planning has been carried out, the computer can be instructed to analyse the network, carry out resource scheduling (if required) and produce a work-to list for every project department. Examples of work-to lists were given in the previous chapter.

Issuing work schedules: targeting instructions for action

Dissemination of programme information must be made far more effective than simply issuing complete work schedules to all and sundry. Instead each department should receive a work-to list showing only those tasks for which it is directly responsible.

Instructions are often ignored when they are issued to too many people, instead of being targeted only to the person who is expected to arrange for action. If an instruction is issued in a document that goes to several departments, each may do nothing and rely instead on the others to carry the instruction out. This risk exists when project networks or other schedules are distributed to a wide number of departments or people without any explanation or precise instructions. Appropriately filtered work-to lists, on the other hand, possess the advantage of being specific to their addressees, so that management responsibility for each item on each list is the clear responsibility of the recipient.

Work-to lists will probably need to cover only a few weeks ahead, but longer-term summaries may have to be given to help departmental managers to recruit or reserve the necessary people. All of this is readily achievable with the filtering and sorting capabilities of modern project management software.

Work-to lists in relation to departmental work procedures

Work-to lists can be regarded as departmental orders or as planning reminders, depending on the department to which they are sent.

Departmental managers' authority
The instructions or reminders contained in work-to lists should in no way detract from the personal authority vested in each departmental manager.

Although the source of each instruction is the project manager's office, the information should derive from the detailed project plan that was first made, reviewed and agreed by departmental managers. The authority of these managers, far from being undermined, should actually be reinforced. Each manager effectively receives a list of the work required of his or her department, but is free to allocate the work to individuals within the department and to direct and control it. With work-to lists resulting from sensible resource scheduling, there should be no chronic departmental overloads (temporary overloads will always remain a risk). These managers are in fact provided with more effective tools which should help them to control the activities of their particular groups.

Manufacturing
Work-to lists for manufacturing would normally be sent to the production manager or production controller, who would continue to issue works orders, job tickets, route cards or any other form of document demanded by the customary procedures used throughout the manufacturing organization. The levels of detail shown in project networks (and, therefore, in the resulting work-to lists) are bound to be far coarser than those needed for the day-to-day planning and control of factory operations. Work-to lists will probably provide the expected start and required finish dates for each assembly and subassembly. It is highly unlikely that any work-to list derived from project planning would specify a greater degree of work breakdown.

The manufacturing organization will, therefore, use its production engineering, planning and control facilities to interpret drawings, identify the parts and materials required and carry out detailed production scheduling. This must be done to satisfy the dates given on the work-to lists but, if project resource scheduling can be used, the rate of working requested should lie within the capacity of the manufacturing plant.

Engineering design

In engineering design departments, the work-to lists are more likely to be used for controlling day-to-day work without need for the additional documents and procedures required in manufacturing departments.

However, networks are not always drawn with sufficient breakdown detail for the day-to-day allocation of work, and it may still be necessary for managers and supervisors to arrange for very detailed activities to be listed manually. A network activity usually summarizes a group of drawings needed for a small work package or subassembly, and it is not usually desirable or possible to have a separate network activity for every individual project drawing or for every small item to be purchased. Drawing lists or drawing schedules and purchase control schedules or bills of materials are usually required to show the greater level of detail than is possible from the project network diagram.

In many engineering design offices and other software groups, highly qualified staff may be found whose talents are not being exploited to the full. While technical and scientific aims might be well defined and understood, there is always a danger that the associated commercial aspects of time and cost are not sufficiently well known or appreciated. The inclusion of estimated costs and target dates on work-to lists can contribute to the more effective use of highly trained specialists in this type of environment by making them aware of their time and cost responsibilities.

Drawing and purchase control schedules

Drawing schedules (or drawing lists) show all the drawings which have to be made for a project. They can be used for the allocation of drawing numbers provided that such numbers are contained within blocks of numbers reserved in the company's central drawing register. Drawing schedules are specific to the project, whereas the central drawing register is a general company record, listing all drawings made for all purposes.

Purchase schedules list all items of equipment to be purchased for a project and are used to allocate technical specification serial numbers (and possibly enquiry, requisition and purchase order numbers too). They are to the large project what the parts list or bill of materials is to a small manufacturing project.

When the project is finished, the drawing and purchase control schedules (which will almost certainly be held in computer files) must show all the final drawing numbers with their correct revisions, and all the purchase specification numbers and their final revisions. The schedules will then define the 'as-built' condition of the project.

9

Purchasing

Purchasing is part of a wider materials management function that might include vendor appraisal, contract negotiation, goods inwards inspection and the safe handling and storage of goods received. It extends beyond the boundaries of the purchaser's premises to embrace supervisory expediting and inspection visits to suppliers, packing and transport arrangements, port and customs' clearance for international movements, and involvement whenever special provisions have to be made for insurance, credit guarantees and other commercial arrangements.

Methods and procedures will depend to some extent on the type of industry and the nature of the goods being purchased. At one end of the scale is the urgent item of stationery obtained by sending someone to the nearest high street shop with petty cash. At the other extreme is the purchase of a complete piece of complex capital plant or an enormous bulk purchase of materials. Figure 9.1 charts the more common functions of purchasing against order value and complexity. This chapter describes some of the activities that lie towards the middle column of this chart, concerned with purchasing materials, components, equipment and services of moderate value.

Efficient purchasing is essential for the success of any industrial

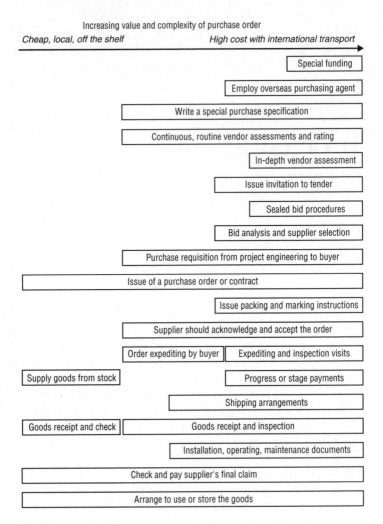

Increasing value and complexity of purchase order

Cheap, local, off the shelf   *High cost with international transport*

Special funding

Employ overseas purchasing agent

Write a special purchase specification

Continuous, routine vendor assessments and rating

In-depth vendor assessment

Issue invitation to tender

Sealed bid procedures

Bid analysis and supplier selection

Purchase requisition from project engineering to buyer

Issue of a purchase order or contract

Issue packing and marking instructions

Supplier should acknowledge and accept the order

Order expediting by buyer | Expediting and inspection visits

Supply goods from stock | Progress or stage payments

Shipping arrangements

Goods receipt and check | Goods receipt and inspection

Installation, operating, maintenance documents

Check and pay supplier's final claim

Arrange to use or store the goods

Figure 9.1   Typical purchasing procedures

project. Delays caused by materials shortages or purchasing errors can be very damaging to a project, causing work interruption, delays and expensive idle time. Perhaps a good way to emphasize the importance of purchasing and materials control is to remember that purchased goods and services account for over half the total costs of many projects.

In this chapter the word 'buyer' is used to describe the person or group responsible directly for the purchasing function. This might be a purchasing agent, purchasing manager or a suitably experienced buying clerk in a purchasing department.

Listing and specifying the goods

The first step in purchasing is for the project engineer to list and then specify the materials needed.

Listing

Listing is carried out either on parts lists or on purchase control schedules, both probably held in computer files. The two methods are similar and simply require the engineer to list each item, give the quantity required and add a description and a specification or catalogue number. The correct revision status of all specifications must be given.

Specifying

Sometimes a relevant national standards specification (for example a British Standards Specification) will exist that can be quoted to specify the requirements of a purchase. There are also many specifications provided by other official bodies, including the armed services.

Bought-out parts, equipment and materials can often be specified by reference to a manufacturer's catalogue or part number. This would appear to be a sufficiently rigid description of the goods. It has to be remembered, however, that most manufacturers reserve the right to modify their designs. If goods are supplied by a stockist, that supplier might decide to restock from more than one manufacturer, and there might be significant differences in quality or even design.

Some companies take no chances and produce their own drawings and specifications and allocate part numbers themselves. This practice costs a considerable amount of engineering time, but has much to commend it. Apart from removing any ambiguity about what is being ordered, provision is thus made for a common part-numbering system, which simplifies stock-handling and purchasing procedures and eases the burden of the cost office. For complex components or specially manufactured equipment, the project engineers must write a detailed purchase specification.

Early ordering of long-lead items

Engineers and others responsible for initiating project purchases have a duty to identify those items that are likely to have long lead times and ensure that ordering instructions are passed to the purchasing department as soon as possible. This may mean issuing advance information on such things as special bearings, motors and other bought-out components, although the relevant assembly drawings and final bills of material remain unfinished or even unstarted.

It is sometimes desirable to issue advance information even when the goods cannot be specified in exact detail, because this gives the purchasing department the chance to get started on obtaining provisional quotations and (in a really urgent case) on reserving capacity in a manufacturer's works by issuing a letter of intent. Any company with sufficient project experience will attempt to follow such practices as a matter of course. Planning a project using a critical path network will almost certainly highlight any need to issue advance purchasing instructions.

Supplier selection

The buyer's first responsibility is to select a suitable source of supply. Occasionally only one supplier can be found, or one may be specified on the requisition written by the project engineers. Limitation of choice usually arises when goods are highly specialized but, even where there is only one manufacturer, there may be a choice between different stockists.

There are, of course, occasions when urgency is the most important factor, when there is simply no time in which to conduct a proper supplier selection procedure. In all other cases, the supplier should be chosen after the collection and perusal of several competitive quotations.

Purchase enquiries

Whenever competitive quotations are required, the engineers must assist the buyer to compile a bid package. This will include the technical specification and commercial needs of the project. The engineers might have a preferred supplier or a short list of possible suppliers, and frequently the buyer will know of others who should be approached.

Obtaining bids
The degree of formality observed during the bidding process will depend to a large extent on the value of the item being ordered. For most routine cases, the purchaser will attempt to collect bids that give price and delivery on a comparable basis, allowing a bid summary form to be completed (see Figure 9.2). For high cost items these procedures are often very rigid, with strict procedures governing the issue of an invitation to tender (ITT) and methods for receiving and assessing the resulting bids. Large purchases and contracts for projects in the public sector are also subject to special regulations within the EU: these specify arrangements for issuing notices in the *European Journal*, so that all relevant suppliers within the EU are made aware of the opportunities and given a chance to bid.

Special requirements when purchases have to be shipped
When a bidder must ship goods to an overseas site, the boundaries of responsibility for transportation must be clearly defined in bids and on purchase orders. Incoterms, defined and published by the International Chamber of Commerce, are accepted worldwide as the succinct and definitive method for setting out these boundaries. Full definitions of these terms are given in ICC Publication 460 (see the select bibliography at the end of this book).

Bid summary
Bearing in mind that potential suppliers might be in different countries, using different national currencies, the buyer should

attempt to obtain enough information with each bid to allow true price and delivery comparison. That means calculating the effective delivery time from the supplier's premises to the project site, and the total delivered cost including all freight, duty and other charges. A form such as that shown in Figure 9.2 might be used. All costs should be converted to the same currency, to allow like-for-like comparison.

In many cases there will be dialogue or negotiation between bidders and the buyer during the bidding period. These aspects are not discussed here, but they can obviously influence the final bids for price and delivery. It is important not to give any supplier an unfair advantage during such discussions by revealing information not available to the other competitors: a standard invitation to tender procedure will usually ensure that a query from one bidder and the buyer's answer will be made known to all the other bidders.

The buyer would normally be expected to favour the lowest bidder, but this choice must be tempered by knowledge of that bidder's reputation for quality, delivery performance and commercial standing. It is usually undesirable and risky to allow the buyer to choose a supplier without the knowledge and agreement of the relevant project engineer.

Ordering

Purchase requisition

Actual authority for the buyer to make a purchase is often initiated by the issue of a purchase requisition to the buyer by the project engineer.

For purchases of significant size or complexity, the requisition will comprise two parts:

1 The technical specification, which the buyer will forward to the chosen supplier with the purchase order.

2 The commercial specification, which sets out the commercial requirements. Some of these might include confidential comments or instructions from the engineer to the buyer, not intended for passing on to the chosen supplier.

BID SUMMARY							
SELLERS ⟶		A	B	C	D	E	F
Country of origin							
Bid reference							
Bid date							
Period of validity							
Bid currency							
Project exchange rate							
Item	Qty	Description	Price	Price	Price	Price	Price	Price
Total quoted ex-works							
Discounts (if any)							
Packing and export prep cost							
Shipping cost							
Customs duty and tax							
Local transport cost							
Estimated total cost on site							
Delivery time ex-works							
Estimated total transport time							
Total delivery time to site							

RECOMMENDED BY THE PURCHASING AGENT:

....
For purchasing agent

RECOMMENDED BY THE ENGINEER:

....
Project/senior engineer

RECOMMENDATION TO THE CLIENT:

....
Project manager

Specification
title:

Specification
number:

Figure 9.2   Bid summary form

Purchase orders

Preparation and issue
Issuing the purchase order is the most routine and obvious part of the purchasing function. Typically, it involves completing a purchase order form, signing it and mailing it to the supplier, together with any supporting drawings and the technical specification. A standard purchase order form should normally be used. This process is sometimes carried out electronically using electronic data interchange (EDI).

The information to be given on a purchase order usually comprises:

1   A purchase order serial number, for identification, filing and possible subsequent information retrieval.
2   The name of the goods to be supplied.
3   The quantity required.
4   The agreed purchase price, as quoted by the supplier and accepted by the purchaser.
5   The delivery date required.
6   The reference number and date of the supplier's quotation or catalogue (if any).
7   The address to which the goods are to be delivered.
8   The terms on which delivery are to be made (liability for transport, packing, insurance costs and so on).
9   Invoicing instructions.
10 An authorizing signature.

What has all this clerical action to do with project management? Part of the answer lies in the time taken. Several days or even weeks of valuable project time can be consumed by this mundane, simple activity. The critical path network must always allow time for the preparation and issue of purchase orders. Unless emergency measures are contemplated, two weeks should often be regarded as a minimum estimate for purchase lead time, even for items that can be supplied from a supplier's stock.

Contractual conditions
The other aspect that should concern the project manager is that each purchase order sets out commercial conditions that, once

accepted by the supplier as a contract, commit the buyer (and therefore the project) to all implied cost and legal implications. It is customary for companies to standardize their usual commercial conditions of purchase and print them on the reverse of their purchase order forms.

After receiving the purchase order, the chosen supplier will be expected to return an acknowledgement accepting the terms, or at least confirming details of quantity, description, price and delivery. Naturally these details must be compared with the supplier's original quotation, and the buyer will question any discrepancy. When the order has been accepted by the supplier, a binding legal contract exists.

Purchase order amendments
Should it become necessary to change any aspect of a purchase order after issue, the supplier's agreement should be sought to determine the effect on price and delivery, and to ensure that the proposed change is within the supplier's capability. Once these facts have been successfully established, an amendment to the original purchase order must be issued.

Each purchase order amendment should bear the same reference number as the original purchase order, suffixed by an identifying amendment number (amendment 1, 2, 3 and so on). Purchase order amendments should be prepared on official forms, and each of these must be given the same distribution as the relevant original purchase order.

Expediting

As far as the purchaser is concerned, the period which follows the issue of a purchase order will be one of waiting, and a great deal of reliance will have to be placed on the supplier to meet its obligations. That is not to say that the purchaser can do nothing. This is the time when the company's expediter can earn his or her money by keeping the supplier reminded of its obligations. Expediting also provides an early warning system, revealing any difficulties which the supplier might be experiencing.

If a satisfactory reply to a routine expediting enquiry is not received, considerable activity is needed from the purchasing department. Their special efforts should not stop until the supplier has either shown the necessary improvement or actually delivered the goods.

Alternative sourcing

When expediting appears to be failing, the design engineers might be able to suggest an alternative item that can be obtained more quickly. The solution might instead mean finding another source of supply. If the original order does have to be cancelled because the supplier has failed to make the agreed delivery, there should be no question of penalties, because the supplier has broken the contract by failing to perform.

Goods receipt

Receipt of the goods is not the end of the story. The consignment must be examined on receipt to check for possible loss or damage in transit. There might also have been some mistake, either in the quantity supplied or in the nature of the goods. Goods inwards inspectors may wish to examine the goods more thoroughly to ensure that they comply with requirements although, in recent years, the tendency has been to place more reliance on the suppliers' own quality procedures.

If the goods are accepted, the goods inwards personnel will record the consignment, usually by distributing copies of a goods inwards certificate. One copy of the certificate will go to the accounts department, which needs it before it can allow payment of the supplier's invoice. Another copy will go to the buying department, to cut short any further expediting action and close off the file on that particular order. Routeing of other copies might include other departments such as the stores, but this depends on the nature of the firm and the goods.

If for any reason the consignment is not received in satisfactory condition, it will be sent smartly back whence it came accompanied by a rejection note. Distribution of rejection notes generally follows that of acceptance certificates, but will produce opposite reactions from the various recipients. For example, the accounts department will not pay any resulting invoice, and the purchasing department will redouble its expediting efforts.

Shortages

Jobs are sometimes delayed because of materials shortages or have to be started before all the necessary materials have been assembled. This can happen if, in spite of expediting, a supplier has failed to deliver on time. Shortages also arise through breakages, theft, inadequate general stock levels, purchasing mistakes and a variety of other reasons.

No project manager likes to see any job delayed because of shortages, and no one wants to start a task before being assured that all the materials are available to carry it through to the finish. Shortages do, however, occur in projects and the method often used to deal with them depends on the issue of shortage lists. These documents can be used on any project – for factory materials or for shortages on a construction site.

Shortage lists

A shortage list form must:

- be quick and simple for the manager or supervisor of the job affected to use;
- describe the missing materials by type and quantity; and
- provide precise, unambiguous information to the person responsible for purchasing so that the purchase order can be identified, allowing the supplier to be contacted.

In addition, a shortage list system should:

- indicate the degree of urgency; and
- allow information feedback, so that the manager or supervisor involved can be told when to expect delivery.

The essential elements of a shortage list are illustrated in Figure 9.3, which is a general purpose form. In practice the storekeeper, supervisor or manager who discovers that there are shortages on a job would fill out a shortage list and despatch it to the relevant buyer by the quickest available means (fax or e-mail if the office is remote).

The shortage list form could be designed so that a copy can be annotated by the buyer and returned to the originator to report back on what is being done to clear the shortages.

Procedures for assuring quality and progress

Suppliers' procedures

The manufacture of each item of special capital equipment is itself an industrial project, demanding (on a smaller scale) project management techniques similar to those used on the main project. A feature of project equipment purchasing is that the buyer will take a detailed interest in the vendor's own project management and quality procedures.

Several large companies and government departments insist that those who supply them with project equipment or carry out subcontracts at least use critical path analysis, and they will probably be expected to show that their quality policy and procedures satisfy the requirements of the international standard ISO 9000 series. It is not unknown for purchasers to offer advice to vendors in establishing their own internal systems.

Inspection and expediting visits

The buyer might wish to arrange visits to a supplier's premises to check on progress, inspect workmanship or witness tests. Such visits could be linked to the certification of stage payments.

There are several ways in which responsibility for carrying out inspection and expediting visits can be allocated or delegated. Where suitable engineers are available to the purchase agent concerned, it is often convenient for the agent to arrange visits which combine the inspection and estimating functions.

Shortage list	Project:				Date issued:
	Department:				Issued by:

To the purchasing manager. The items listed below have not been received and are critical to progress. Please expedite and report as soon as possible.

Order no. (if known)	Description of materials or equipment	Quantity needed	When needed	Reply from purchasing manager	Is work held up?

Figure 9.3 Shortage list

177

Quality and progress reports

The project manager and the client might request a formal quality and progress report from the relevant purchasing agent following each visit to a supplier. The inspecting engineer or expediter will probably be asked to use a convenient standard summary form for this purpose, an example of which is given in Figure 9.4.

Vendors' documents

Provision must usually be made for the project engineers to receive and approve documents from the supplier for machinery or equipment which is manufactured specially for the project. The term 'vendors' documents' is usually applied, although the providers of the goods might also be referred to as manufacturers, sellers, suppliers or subcontractors.

The first step in ensuring the timely receipt of vendors' documents is to make certain that the obligation to provide them is spelled out clearly on the purchase orders or purchase specifications.

When the equipment is delivered, a final set of drawings, certified test results, operating and maintenance manuals and a recommended spares holding list will probably be needed. In some cases, suppliers might be required to supply all these documents translated into a foreign language, according to the nationality of the project end-user.

Foundation, capacity and installation drawings

In addition to general layout or assembly drawings, there is usually a requirement for the early receipt of installation instructions. With heavy plant and machinery, for example, foundation drawings, power supply requirements and overall weights and dimensions are all vital information, the lack of which could hold up work on the project. Obtaining such information, and progressing any necessary approvals, is all part of the expediting process.

INSPECTION/EXPEDITING REPORT				
Report number	Sheet 1 of	Date this visit	Date of last visit	Inspector/expediter

MAIN SUPPLIER DETAILS

Name _____

Address _____

_____

Supplier's reference _____

Persons contacted _____

_____

Equipment _____

_____

_____

_____

Contract delivery date _____

Current delivery estimate _____

Plans for next visit

Date _____

To expedite ☐

To continue inspection ☐

Final inspection ☐

To inspect packing ☐

SUB-SUPPLIER DETAILS

Main supplier's order number _____

Name _____

Address _____

_____

Sub-supplier's reference _____

Persons contacted _____

_____

Equipment _____

_____

_____

Agreed delivery to supplier _____

Current delivery estimate _____

Plans for next visit

Date _____

To expedite ☐

To continue inspection ☐

Final inspection ☐

To inspect packing ☐

ORDER STATUS SUMMARY (see attached sheets for details)

Assessed progress by (weeks)	Tests witnessed?	Complies with spec.?	Released for packing?	Released for shipping?
Early ☐	Yes ☐	Yes ☐	Yes ☐	Yes ☐
Late ☐ _____	No ☐	No ☐	No ☐	No ☐

ACTION REQUIRED	ACTION BY	
	Specification no.	Revision
Title	Purchase order no.	Amendment

Figure 9.4   Inspection and expediting report

Retention of vendors' documents

The project engineering company will have obligations to provide a back-up service to the client after project handover. These obligations usually extend beyond the initial guarantee period and can involve the provision of advice or services in maintaining, repairing, replacing, operating, modifying or extending plant provided for the original project.

Since much of the plant will incorporate equipment purchased from third party suppliers, the company must be able to find and consult any relevant vendor document for many years after project completion. The contractor will therefore need to keep a complete project set of vendors' documentation safely in its own files or archives (either in their original paper state or on some other medium of suitable quality and durability).

It is not sufficient to rely on being able to obtain additional or replacement copies from all the various suppliers in the future. The commercial world is a volatile place. Some original suppliers might lose or destroy their records, be swallowed up in mergers or take-overs, or simply cease trading.

Shipping, port and customs formalities

Marking and labelling

The purchasing agent must ensure that every consignment is properly marked before it leaves the supplier's premises. The marking method required should be stated on the purchase specification and will usually involve suppliers stencilling easily recognizable markings on packing crates so that each item can be clearly identified through all stages of its journey and, not least, by the site personnel when it finally arrives. The purchase order number usually has to be included in all markings.

Freight forwarding agents

It is best to entrust arrangements for long-distance transport, shipping, airfreight, and seaport, airport and international frontier formalities to a specialist organization. The purchasing agent will undoubtedly have considerable experience and expertise, but the employment of a reputable freight forwarding agent will be invaluable.

Freight forwarding agents operate through worldwide organizations. Their staff or representatives are stationed at most of the world's ports and airports and, through communication networks, are able to monitor the progress of every consignment through all stages from initial loading to final delivery.

Collaboration between the purchasing agent and a freight forwarding agent can achieve benefits from the economy of scale obtained when different consignments are consolidated to make up complete container loads.

The combined expertise of the purchasing and freight forwarding agent can be a great comfort to project staff confronted for the first time with the formidable array of documents associated with the international movement of goods. Failure to get the documentation right first time can lead to delays, the impounding of goods and legally imposed penalties.

Local knowledge provided by the forwarding agent's contacts in the countries along the delivery route can yield important information about the type and capacity of port handling facilities, warning of any unusual congestion or industrial disputes (with suggestions for alternative routes), and details of inland road and rail systems (including size and weight restrictions). For example, the agent in one case was able to prevent an expensive mistake by pointing out that a local railway company operated an unusually short restriction on the maximum length of loads, because the route included tunnels with unusually sharp curves. At another port, the local agents were able to warn about a peculiar security problem, where the local shanty-town inhabitants were always on the lookout for fresh supplies of building timber. If such timber happened to exist in the shape of well-constructed packing crates protecting expensive project equipment standing on the dockside – well, who could blame them?

10

Cost management

Many things can happen during the life of a project to alter the expected rate and magnitude of expenditure. The direction of change is usually upwards. Some of the reasons may be unavoidable or unforeseen but, in many cases, the fault will lie somewhere within the project organization. The principal purpose of cost control is to ensure that no preventable wastage of money or unauthorized increase in costs is allowed to happen.

A common misconception is to confuse cost *reporting* with cost *control*. Cost management comprises both reporting and control. Accurate and timely cost reporting is essential but, by itself, is not cost control. By the time overspending is reported, the damage has been done. Cost control must be exercised at the time when the costs are being committed.

A checklist of cost management factors

1   Cost awareness by those responsible for design and engineering.

2   Cost awareness by all other project participants throughout the life of the project.

3   A project work breakdown which yields work packages of manageable size.

4   Cost budgets, divided so that each work package is given its own share of the total budget.

5   A code of accounts system which can be aligned with the work breakdown structure.

6   A cost accounting system that can collect and analyse costs as they are incurred and allocate them with minimum delay to their relevant cost codes.

7   A practicable work schedule.

8   Effective management of well-motivated staff to ensure that progress meets or beats the work schedule.

9   A method for comparing expenditure with that planned for the work actually done.

10   Effective supervision and quality control of all activities aimed at getting things right first time.

11   Proper drafting of specifications and contracts.

12   Discreet investigation to confirm that the customer is of sound financial standing, with sufficient funds available to make all contracted payments.

13   Similar investigation, not necessarily so discreet, of all significant suppliers and subcontractors new to the contractor's experience.

14   Effective use of competitive tendering for all purchases and subcontractors to ensure the lowest costs commensurate with quality and to avoid committing costs that would exceed estimates and budgets.

15   Appropriate consideration and control of modifications and contract variations, including the passing of justifiable claims for price increases on to the customer.

16   Avoidance, where possible, of unbudgeted dayworks on construction contracts.

17   Where dayworks are unavoidable, proper authorization, retention and administration of dayworks sheets.

18   Strict control of payments to suppliers and subcontractors to ensure that all invoices and claims for progress payments are neither overpaid nor paid too soon.

19   Recovery from the customer of all incidental expenses allowed

for in the contract charging structure (for example expensive telephone calls, printing, travel and accommodation).

20 Proper invoicing to the customer, especially ensuring that claims for progress payments or cost reimbursement are made at the appropriate times and at the correct levels, so that disputes do not justify the customer delaying payments.

21 Effective credit control to expedite overdue payments from the customer.

22 Occasional internal security audits to prevent losses through theft or fraud.

23 Effective and regular reports of progress and costs to senior management, highlighting potential schedule or budget overruns in time for corrective action to be taken.

Cost budgets

The initial project budgets must be derived from the cost estimates used when the tender or internal project proposal was prepared. The final version of these become the authorized levels of expenditure for all departments engaged on the project. It is not only the top budget limits that are important, but also the rate at which expenditure is scheduled to take place. When plotted as a graph against time, the typical cumulative project expenditure describes an S curve (see Figure 10.3, for example).

The total budget should spread over the project work breakdown structure so that there is a specified budget for each work package. For true measurement and control, each budget element must correspond to an identifiable and measurable work package. Each of these budget elements and its associated work package must share a unique cost code against which manpower time sheet data, material costs and all other direct expenses can be collected and accumulated. Work breakdown and coding according to these principles was described in Chapter 4.

Labour budgets

Managers and supervisors should be given their work budgets in terms of man-hours rather than as the resulting costs of wages and overheads. The argument is that a manager should never be held accountable for meeting targets where he or she has no authority to control the causal factors. Project managers are rarely responsible for wage and salary levels or company overhead expenses. They can, however, be held accountable for the time taken to complete each work package.

Budgets for purchases and subcontracts

Budgets for purchases and for subcontracts have to be expressed in the appropriate project currency. Relevant packaging, transport, insurance, duties and tax must be included.

Budget changes

Budgets on most projects are not static. They increase each time a customer-requested change results in an agreed increase in the project price. At any time it should be possible for the budget to be stated in terms of its initial amount, additions subsequently approved by the client and, therefore, the total current budget. If possible, these changes should be made at work package level.

Budget adjustments for below-the-line allowances

If the project lasts more than a few months, cost escalation and (for international projects) foreign exchange fluctuations may have to be taken into account in budgets, cost reporting and control.

Any relevant allowances made in the original project estimate for cost escalation, exchange rate fluctuations and contingencies, provided these have been built into the pricing or charging structure, can be regarded as 'reserve budgets'. Appropriate sums can be 'drawn down' from these reserves from time to time to augment the control budget.

Purchased materials, equipment and services

The costs of bought-out supplies and services are ordained when the purchase orders are negotiated and issued. This might be a long time before the goods are actually received and issued. Purchasing cost control can only be exercised, therefore, when each order is being placed. Once an order has been issued, the costs are committed. If the total price exceeds the amount budgeted for the particular item, it is simply too late to do anything about it.

Any subsequent purchasing cost control procedures can only contribute to cost control in the sense that they will indicate adverse trends as early as possible. If poor purchasing performance has been experienced early in the project, the best that can be done is to ensure that an improvement takes place before or when the remaining orders are committed.

Cumulative expenditure graphs

A curve can be plotted to show the cumulative value of purchase orders as they are placed. This is a curve of committed expenditure which can be compared with the original budget.

Any curve showing materials commitments will be far more useful if a budget comparison curve is first plotted on the same axes, like a track along which the committed expenditure is expected to run as the points are plotted. The points for plotting the timed budget curve must be calculated by adding together the materials cost estimates for each task and timing them according to the dates when the orders are scheduled to be issued, not forgetting to include the value of any common stock items that are to be drawn from stores.

Including milestones on the graph (as described later in this chapter) will enhance its value.

Tabulation showing predicted final project purchasing costs

A more accurate approach to monitoring purchasing cost performance is to tabulate actual cumulative project purchasing costs against the estimates for the corresponding items or work packages.

If this is done at regular intervals a pattern will emerge which shows, for all the orders committed to date, whether any trend towards over- or under-spending is emerging. The experience gained can be used in carrying out regular reviews of the cost estimates for all goods yet to be ordered. This will allow regular predictions to be made of the total materials expenditure, so that these can be compared with the authorized budgets for updating the forecast project profitability.

Where it is intended to use this method to make a continually improving prediction of the final cost, four sets of data have to be gathered and tabulated:

1   The total cost of all orders already placed.
2   The total estimated cost of all purchase orders yet to be placed.
3   The cost of any materials already issued from general stock.
4   The estimated cost of any materials still to be used from general stock.

Milestone analysis

Milestone analysis is one of the simpler methods which managers can use throughout the project life cycle to compare the actual costs and progress experienced with the costs and progress planned. The method is less effective than detailed earned value analysis (outlined later in this chapter) but it has the merit of needing a relatively modest amount of management effort to set up and maintain. It also requires less sophisticated cost accounting than other methods and can be used when project schedules are not particularly detailed.

Identifying milestones

The first requirement in milestone analysis is to understand what is meant by a milestone. Milestones are selected key activities or events that lie at the boundaries between significant phases of the project. Put another way, a milestone denotes a particular, easily recognized stage in the progress of a project towards completion. It might be acceptance by the customer of a final design concept, the issue of a package of drawings, the day when a building is made watertight so that internal trades can start or any other such occasion.

Milestone analysis starts, therefore, by choosing and naming the events that can most effectively be used as project milestones. Ideally, milestones should coincide with the completion of packages from the work breakdown structure. That approach will be assumed in the remainder of this discussion.

Plotting the budget/milestone plan

For each milestone, two pieces of data are required:

1   The date on which the milestone is scheduled to be achieved.
2   The estimated cost or budget for the associated work package (that is, the expected cost of all the work needed to achieve the milestone).

With all milestone data available, the milestone/budget curve can be plotted. The curve of budgeted expenditure is built up cumulatively, by adding the cost estimates for the work necessary to achieve each milestone, taking care that the grand total is equal to the total project cost budget and that no cost estimates are left out.

The date for each milestone is found by reference to the project schedule. Then, with the planned time and cost data available for each milestone, a symbol can be drawn on the budget curve that will show both the planned cost and scheduled date for every milestone in the project.

If desired and (more significantly) if the data and willingness to spend the time are available, a separate milestone chart could be drawn for each department, complemented by the total chart for the project.

Plotting the graph of actual expenditure and milestone achievement

To be able to plot the graph of actual expenditure for comparison against the plan, two further items of information must be collected:

1   The date on which each milestone was actually achieved.
2   The project costs actually incurred (including committed costs of purchased items) at the end of each cost monitoring period.

It must, therefore, be assumed that a procedure exists for recording the total costs actually incurred or committed for the project at suitable intervals. These intervals might be weekly or monthly and will depend to some extent on the total life cycle time for the project.

The actual costs can be plotted as a graph on the same axes as the graph of budgeted costs. Points on the graph should be highlighted by symbols to indicate the actual completion date for each milestone. To be able to compare the planned and actual graphs sensibly, it helps enormously if all the milestones can be given simple numbers. If the milestones marked on the budget curve are, for example, numbered 1, 2, 3, 4 and so on, the corresponding points on the actual graph can carry the same numbers to make comparison easy.

A milestone analysis example

A construction project expected to last just over one year is the basis for this example. The dotted curve in Figure 10.2 shows the time-scaled budget for the project, drawn by combining data from the project schedule and the authorized cost estimates. Thirteen milestones have been identified for the project, and the planned schedule and cost data for these are tabulated in Figure 10.1.

Each milestone has been indicated on the planned curve by placing a circle at the time when it should be achieved. The

	Milestone description	Schedule (week number)		Cumulative cost £(1000s)	
		Plan	Actual	Budget	Actual
1	Project start authorized	0	6	0	0
2	Design approved	12	14	25	20
3	Drawings issued for building	16	18	60	55
4	Foundations completed	20	22	100	100
5	Drawings issued for services	24	26	180	180
6	All equipment for services ordered	26	28	275	290
7	Walls built to eaves	28	30	345	385
8	Windows and doors finished	32		500	
9	Roof on, building watertight	36		630	
10	Wiring and plumbing finished	40		730	
11	Services installed and tested	44		795	
12	Internal finishes completed	48		825	
13	Site and building handover	56		845	

Figure 10.1   Data for milestone example

numbers within the circles are codes that identify the particular milestones.

Monitoring method
Actual cost and progress data have been gathered up to the end of week 30 for this project and these are included in the tabulated data shown in Figure 10.1. The results have been plotted, at two-weekly intervals, as the solid line curve in Figure 10.2. Any milestone passed during each two-weekly period has been indicated on the actual cost curve by means of a diamond containing the milestone's identification number.

Interpreting the results
Of course, if all is going exactly according to plan, the budget and actual graphs should lie together on the same path and the milestone points should coincide. When they do not, investigation should give some indication of the project cost and achievement performance to date.

Imagine that you are the general manager of the construction company responsible for this project and that it has been running for just over eight weeks. You have been given a copy of the milestone chart by the project manager. If you look at week 8 on Figure 10.2 you will see that milestone 1, project start, has been achieved six weeks late, as indicated by the position of the diamond compared with the circle. The very low costs recorded at week 8 indicate that little or no activity is taking place. So, you can easily see that the project has started late and that more effort is needed urgently if progress is to catch up with the plan.

When you receive your updated milestone chart at the end of week 14 it tells you that milestone 2 has now been reached. It should have happened at week 12, but the project has been pulled up from being six weeks late to only two weeks late. Costs recorded up to week 14 are £20 000. These costs compare against a budget of £25 000 for achieving milestone 2. Expenditure at week 14 should have reached about £45 000 (the dotted curve). So you conclude that the project is still running slightly late and that the rate of expenditure is lower than plan so extra effort is needed. You are, however, getting value for the money spent because milestone 2 was achieved for £5000 less than its estimated cost.

If you continue to observe the chart at consecutive two-weekly

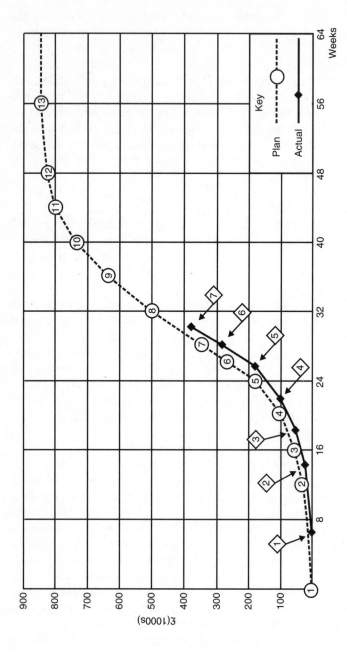

Figure 10.2 Comparing project cost and achievement using milestones

intervals, you can see how it depicts the changing trend. In particular, the cost performance gradually deteriorates. One significant report from the project manager is the milestone chart updated to the end of week 28. The graphs indicate that milestone 6 should have been achieved at week 26 for a project cost of £275 000. You can see from the graphs, however, that milestone 6 has only just been reached at week 28 at a cost of £290 000. So the project is not only still running two weeks late but also running £15 000 over budget.

By week 30, it is apparent that the project programme, as indicated by milestone 7, continues to run two weeks late, and the costs at £385 000 have risen to £40 000 over the corresponding budget for milestone 7.

Without the milestones as measuring points, none of this analysis would have been possible.

Need for replotting
If, for example, a change in project scope causes rescheduling of work or costs, then the data for future milestones will obviously change too. The curve of predicted expenditure and milestone will have to be amended at each significant authorized change so that it remains up to date and a true basis for comparison of actual costs against plan.

A simple performance analysis method for design engineering

Most projects start their lives in a design department. The easiest approach is to determine how many drawings and specifications are to be produced and then divide this number into the number of drawings and specifications actually issued, multiply the answer by one hundred and declare this as the percentage of design completed.

Although some companies actually use this method, it is far too crude because it fails to take into account all the conceptual design work needed and assumes that the work involved in producing one drawing is equivalent to the amount of work needed to produce any other drawing. The method can, however, be used in limited cases, such as for a department which is producing a large number of similar electrical running diagrams or piping and instrumentation diagrams.

An outline of earned value analysis

Earned value analysis can be regarded as the missing link between cost reporting and cost control. It depends on the existence of a sound framework of planning and control, including the following:

- A detailed work breakdown structure.
- A correspondingly detailed cost coding system.
- Timely and accurate collection and reporting of cost data.
- A method for monitoring and quantifying the amount of work done, including work in progress.

The earned value process aims to compare the costs incurred for an accurately identified amount of work with the costs budgeted for that same work. It can be applied at the level of individual tasks or complete work packages and the data are usually rolled up for the whole project. The procedure uses the results to produce a cost performance index. If everything is going exactly according to plan the cost performance index will be 1.0. An index less than 1.0 indicates that the value earned for the money being spent is less than that expected.

Earned value nomenclature and definitions

The following are a few of the names and abbreviations used in earned value analysis. The list is far from complete but includes most commonly used quantities.

BCWS   Budgeted cost of work scheduled. This is the budget or cost estimate for work scheduled to be complete at the measurement date. It corresponds with the time-scaled budget.

BCWP   Budgeted cost of work performed. This is the amount

of money or labour time that the amount of work actually performed at the measurement date should have cost to be in line with the budget or cost estimate. It is usually necessary to take into account work that is in progress in addition to tasks actually completed.

ACWP   Actual cost of the work performed – at the measurement date.

CPI   Cost performance index. This indicates the measure of success in achieving results against budget. Anything less than unity indicates that the value earned from money spent is less than that intended.

SPI   Schedule performance index. This can be used as a measure of progress performance against plan, but is less commonly used than the CPI. Anything less than unity shows progress slower than that planned.

These quantities can be used in the following expressions:

$$CPI = \frac{BCWP}{ACWP}$$

$$SPI = \frac{BCWP}{BCWS}$$

Brick wall project: a simple example of earned value analysis

For this example of earned value analysis I have chosen a project comprising one main activity for which progress can be measured quantitatively without difficulty or ambiguity.

Imagine a bricklayer and a labourer engaged in building a new boundary wall enclosing a small country estate. If the amount of progress made had to be assessed at any time, work achieved could be measured in terms of the area of wall built or, more simply here, by the length of wall finished.

The scope, budget and schedule for this project have been defined by the following data:

● Total length of wall to be built = 1000 m.
● Estimated total project cost = £40 000.

- Planned duration for the project is 10 weeks, with 5 working days in each week = 50 days.
- The rate of progress is expected to be uniform and linear.

When the above data are considered, the following additional facts emerge:

- Budget cost per day = £800.
- Planned rate of building = 20 m of wall per day.
- Budget cost for each metre of wall finished = £40.

At the end of day 20 the project manager has been asked to carry out an earned value analysis. The actual and planned data for the end of day 20 are as follows:

- Work performed: 360 m of wall have been completed.
- ACWP (actual cost of work performed): £18 000. This is the total project cost at the end of day 20.
- BCWS (budget cost of work scheduled): 20 days at £800 per day = £16 000.
- BCWP (budget cost of work performed): 360 m of wall should have cost £40 per metre or £14 400.

Cost implications
The cost implications of these data can be analysed using earned value analysis as follows:

$$\text{Cost performance index (CPI)} = \frac{\text{BCWP}}{\text{ACWP}} = \frac{14\,400}{18\,000} = 0.8$$

The implication of this for final project cost can be viewed in at least two ways.

1 We could divide the original estimate of £40 000 by the cost performance index and say that the predicted total project cost has risen to £50 000, which gives a projected cost variance of £10 000 for the project.
2 Alternatively, we can say that £18 000 has been spent to date and then work out the likely remaining cost. The 360 m of wall built so far have actually cost £18 000, which is a rate of £50 per metre. The amount of work remaining is 640 m of wall and, if

this should also cost £50 per metre, that will mean a further £32 000 predicted cost remaining to completion. So, adding costs measured to date and remaining costs predicted to completion again gives an estimated total cost at project completion of £50 000.

Schedule implications
Earned value data can be used to predict the likely completion date for an activity or a project, although a straightforward comparison of progress against the plan is likely to be an easier and more effective method. If the earned value method is used, the first step is to calculate the schedule performance index. For the wall project at day 20 the SPI is found by:

$$\text{SPI} = \frac{\text{BCWP}}{\text{BCWS}} = \frac{14\,400}{16\,000} = 0.9$$

The original estimate for the duration of this project was 50 working days. Dividing by the SPI gives a revised total project duration of about 56 days.

Methods for assessing the progress on a task

Most earned value analysis must be performed not just on one activity, as in the brick wall project just described, but on many project activities. At any given measurement time in a large project, three stages of progress can apply to all the activities. These stages are as follows:

1 Activity not started. Earned value is therefore zero.
2 Activity completed. Earned value is therefore equal to the activity's cost budget.
3 Activity in progress or interrupted. For construction projects, as in the case of the brick wall project, earned value can often be assessed by measuring actual quantities of work done. For other, less tangible tasks, it is necessary to estimate the proportion or percentage of work done, and then take the same proportion of the current authorized cost estimate as the actual value of work performed.

Earned value analysis prediction reliability and implications

Early predictions of final costs always tend to be unreliable. There are at least four reasons for this:

1 Estimates of progress or of work remaining to completion are only judgements and people usually err on the side of optimism.
2 During the first few weeks or even months of a large project, the sample of work analysed in earned value calculations is too small to produce valid indications of later trends.
3 There is no guarantee that the performance levels early in a project, even when they have been accurately assessed, will remain at those same levels throughout the remainder of the project.
4 Although many activities, especially in design, might be declared as 100 per cent completed, it is inevitable that further work will be needed when questions arise as drawings and specifications are put to use in manufacturing or construction. It is quite likely that some drawings will have to be re-issued with corrections or modifications. Unless due allowance has been made elsewhere for this 'after issue' work, the project budget might eventually be exceeded.

What if the prediction is bad?

Suppose the actual hours recorded for a project greatly exceed the earned value, so that the resulting prediction indicates final costs well in excess of the budget. The first thing to be noted is that the project manager should be grateful to this method for producing the earliest possible warning. Escape may be possible even from an apparently hopeless situation, provided that suitable action can be taken in time.

Stricter control of modifications should help to curb unnecessary expenditure and conserve budgets. While changes requested by the customer will be paid for, and so should augment the budget, all other requests for changes must be thoroughly scrutinized before authorization. Only essential unfunded changes should be allowed. Modification control, a very important aspect of project management, is described in Chapter 11.

In the face of vanishing budgets, the demands made on individuals will have to be more stringent, but this can only be achieved through good communications, by letting all the participants know what the position is, what is expected of them and why. It is important to gain their full cooperation. The project manager will find this easiest to achieve within a project team organization. If a matrix organization exists, the project manager must work through all the departmental managers involved to achieve good communications and motivation.

The performance of individuals can often be improved considerably by setting short- and medium-term goals or objectives. These must always be quantifiable, so that the results can be measured objectively, removing any question of favouritism or bias in performance assessment and helping the individual to monitor his or her own performance.

In the project context, these personal objectives must be equated (by means of the work breakdown structure) with the objectives of time, cost and performance for the project as a whole. The three go hand-in-hand and, if work is done on time, the cost objective should be met. Although all the objectives should have been set at the start of a project, they can be reviewed if things are going wrong and budgets appear to be at risk. However, care must be taken not to set objectives that cannot possibly be met.

If, in spite of all efforts, a serious overspend still threatens, there remains the possibility of replenishing the project coffers from their original source – the customer. This feat can sometimes be accomplished by re-opening the fixed price negotiation whenever a suitable opportunity presents itself. An excuse to renegotiate may be provided, for example, if the customer asks for a substantial modification, or as a result of economic factors that are beyond the contractor's control. Failing this step, smaller modifications or project spares can be priced generously in order to offset the areas of loss or low profitability. Care must also be taken that every item that the contract allows to be charged as an expense to the customer is so charged.

Remember that without earned value analysis forewarning of possible overspending may not be received in time to allow any corrective action at all. The project manager must always be examining cost trends, rather than simple historical cost reports. When the predictions are bad, despair is the wrong philosophy. It is far better to carry out a careful reappraisal of the remaining project activities and to explore all possible avenues which might lead to a restoration of the original project profit targets.

Effect of modifications on earned value analysis

Every modification or other change introduced into a project can be expected to have some effect on the level of achievement attained by the departments involved. Before this effect can be measured, one significant question must always be answered:

● Can the customer be held liable for any additional costs or must the additional work be paid for out of the existing budget (and, therefore, out of the potential profits)?

Control of modifications is dealt with in the following chapter. It can be assumed that, long before any modification reaches the stage of implementation, the change committee or other designated authority will have defined every change as 'customer funded' or 'unfunded'.

Unfunded modifications

Each unfunded modification will affect the total workload remaining, usually with no corresponding change to the authorized budgets. In most cases the effect will be to increase the remaining workload, so that the proportion of work achieved is depressed in all the departments affected.

It is possible to make an appropriate correction for unfunded modifications to the achievement measurement for each department. Each modification would have to be added to the task list, along with a cost estimate for the additional work needed. There can, of course, be no corresponding increase in the authorized budget.

Such adjustments are unnecessary, and unfunded modifications can be ignored, provided that:

- they are not too numerous or horrendous; and
- they do not cancel out work already reported as achieved.

Modification costs are often extremely difficult to estimate and record, because of the way in which the work is intermingled with the original task affected. If, for instance, a wiring diagram is changed for a complex piece of equipment, it can be impossible to work out the changed cost of carrying out the wiring task.

Unfunded modifications will therefore show up as apparent overspending, which is, of course, just what they are. Achievement predictions will be self-correcting as these overspends are picked up, even if they are not immediately identifiable as being expressly due to unfunded modifications.

Completed work rendered void by unfunded modifications

Unfunded modifications which nullify work already carried out must always be taken into account by erasure of the relevant achievement from the records. This should be done for every department affected, and either whole tasks or parts of them may have to be reinstated into the remaining workload. In this way, the achievement calculations can be kept on a true course.

Customer-funded modifications

Funded modifications can be considered as new tasks, for addition both to the task list and to its authorized budgets. The customer should be asked to pay for any work which is scrapped as a result of the modification, in which case that work can be considered as having been sold and, therefore, achieved. It need not be subtracted from the achievement tally.

The project ledger concept

A picture has now been built up of a collection of methods by which data can be displayed on graphs or in tables to show the predicted and measured performance against plans and budgets. Although space only allowed a simple brick wall project to be demonstrated, the procedures for other departments and operations in far more complex projects follow the same principles.

Successful budgetary control and cost prediction obviously require a certain amount of accurate book-keeping, not only within the boundaries of the accounts department, but also under the administration of the project manager.

The dossier of achievement returns, estimates and budgets, all collated with respect to the project task list, can be regarded as a project ledger. The ledger account is credited with the initial cost budgets plus any authorized additions, such as those arising from customer-requested modifications and contract variation orders. The value of work achieved, in cost terms, is debited from the ledger as it is reported, to leave a balance outstanding which represents the estimated cost of work remaining. At any time it should be possible to consult the ledger in order to determine the cost/budget/achievement status of every department engaged on the project.

The ledger will most probably be set up in a computer, either in a central management information system or using one of the more powerful project management packages. The method is very difficult to apply successfully because of the difficulty in obtaining and maintaining accurate data.

Predicting profitability for a project

Once a basis has been established for the collection of data for earned value calculations from all parts of the project organization, it is a logical and progressive step to put all these results together to obtain a composite prediction of total project costs.

Of course, the first such prediction is that made before the start of the project, when the initial cost estimates and budgets are prepared and when progress can confidently be declared as zero.

Subsequent analysis and cost prediction can be regarded as a continuous process by which the original estimate is steadily refined. As more work is completed, the total estimate remaining to completion contains an increasing proportion of actual cost data, so that the predictions should become more accurate.

For cost control purposes, these data should be presented in a way that shows up unwanted trends as early as possible, before it becomes too late for anything to be done. Graphical methods can be used (see Figure 10.3) but a computer tabulation method will be described here, as being capable of showing more detail that can more easily be read accurately.

Spreadsheet presentation

Project cost summaries and predictions are commonly presented in tabular or spreadsheet form. Figure 10.4 shows a widely used arrangement, suitable for preparation from purely manual methods or from computer systems. Tables such as this are typically bound into regular cost and progress reports, often produced at monthly intervals.

Column A lists the main project sections from the project work breakdown. The example in Figure 10.4 is taken from an engineering company which referred to these main sections as plant sections. The listing in column A must include all cost items, including software tasks and summarized miscellaneous items. If more detail is required, this can be provided on back-up sheets.

Column B lists the cost code of every main project section. This makes it easier to refer back to the original estimates and budgets and to audit the data presented.

In column C the original budgets for the project sections are shown, and these add up to the total original project budget at the foot of the column. This is the cost budget originally authorized and approved, which should be equal to the original cost estimates. Consideration must be given to the inclusion or otherwise of escalation and other below-the-line estimates, and it may be necessary to add explanatory notes in the accompanying report text.

As the project proceeds, it can be expected that a number of variations or modifications will arise that are agreed with the client, and for which the client will pay. These must obviously increase both the project revenue and the budget. Budget increments from this cause are listed in column D. These, when added to the original budget for each project section, give the current revised authorized budgets (column E).

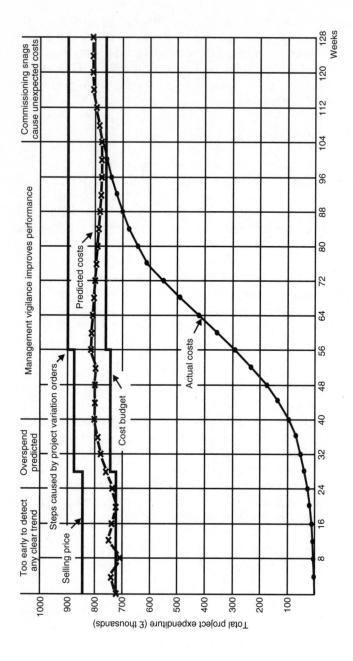

Figure 10.3 A cost and profit prediction graph (shown after project completion)

Project cost report summary

Project title:

Project number:

Page   of

Report date:

A Item	B Cost code	C Original budget	D Authorized budget changes	E Authorized current budget C+D	F ACWP	G BCWP (assessed)	H CPI	J Forecast costs remaining (E–G)/H	K Forecast costs at completion F+J	L Forecast variance at completion E–K

Figure 10.4 A project cost report spreadsheet

In any project of significant size there are usually variations under consideration or awaiting approval that could ultimately affect the budget (and progress assessment). Until such variations have been agreed with the client it is obviously not possible to take the additional revenue for granted. It may, nevertheless, be of considerable interest to know the value of any such proposals which happen to be 'in the pipeline' at the report date. Some people include a column on their report formats to show the costs of these pending variations. This has not been done here owing to limited space.

Column F lists the costs actually recorded as at the report date. In earned value analysis terms these are the actual costs of work performed (ACWP). They comprise the following:

1   All labour hours booked to the project (on time sheets or job tickets) converted at standard cost or other appropriate rates into the project control currency.

2   Overheads and administrative costs.

3   Payments for directly relevant insurance premiums, licences, legal fees and consultants' fees.

4   Payments made to, or legitimately claimed by, subcontractors.

5   The cost of all materials committed, which includes the cost of all materials and equipment already used or delivered, plus the value of all other materials and equipment for which orders have been placed at the report date. In all cases freight, packing, insurance, agents' fees and duties paid or committed must be included.

6   Any other costs incurred or committed up to the report date that can be directly attributed to the project.

Column G in Figure 10.4 is the BCWP, budgeted cost of work performed, which is the assessment of earned value. This is the best assessment of earned value that can be made, taking care to include allowances for work in progress as well as for tasks actually completed.

Column H shows the cost performance index, the factor derived from comparing the figures in columns F and G. This factor is applied to the original budget for the work remaining. The result is a prediction of the likely cost of the work remaining (in column J).

Adding the forecast remaining costs to the actual expenditure to date yields the best possible estimate of what the project final total cost will be (column K). As time passes, the forecast element of this figure will become less, the proportion of actual costs will become greater and the final prediction will grow more accurate.

The final column, L, in Figure 10.4 shows the expected difference between the final project costs and the approved budget.

Post-mortem

When the project is finished and the final costs become known an investigation can be conducted to compare the actual expenditure with the original estimates. Such post-mortem examinations are obviously far too late to be of benefit to the completed project, but they can be helpful in pointing out mistakes to avoid when estimating or conducting future projects.

11

Changes

No commercial project can be expected to run from initial order to final completion without at least one change. Changes can arise from a customer's request, a self-inflicted engineering design modification or through the built project differing in some respect from the officially issued drawings, specifications or other formal instructions.

Classification of changes

Changes can be placed in one of two principal commercial categories. The vital question is: 'Did this change originate inside our own organization or has it come from the customer?' The answer will usually decide whether the change is to be funded by the customer or not.

External, funded changes

Changes requested by the customer automatically imply a corresponding change to the contract, since the specification forms part of the contract documentation. If, as usually happens, the modification results in an increase in the contractor's costs, a suitable change to the contract price must be negotiated. The delivery schedule may also be affected and any resulting delays must be predicted, discussed and agreed.

Customer-funded modifications may possess nuisance value and can disrupt the smooth flow of logically planned work, but they do nevertheless offer the prospect of compensation through an increase in price and profit. When a customer asks for a change, the contractor is in a strong price-bargaining position because there is no competitor.

Internal, unfunded changes

If a contractor finds it necessary to introduce changes itself, the contractor cannot expect the customer to pay unless the change can be attributed to a specific contingency for which provision was made in the contract. The contractor must be prepared to carry the additional costs, write off any work which has to be scrapped and answer to the customer for any resulting delays. For this reason contractors have to be particularly wary about allowing unfunded changes to proceed.

Authorization arrangements

The effects of any change, whether customer-requested or not, may be felt far beyond the confines of the project area that is most obviously and directly affected. This could be true of the technical, timescale or cost aspects. A project has to be regarded as a technical and commercial system, in which a change to one part can react with other parts of the system, bringing about consequences that the change's originator may not have been able to foresee. For these reasons alone it is prudent that every proposed change be considered by at least one key member from each project department, so that the likely effects can be predicted as reliably as possible. Naturally these considerations should take place before any change is put into practice.

The change committee

In many project organizations a regular panel of experts is appointed to consider changes and decide how they are to be handled. Departmental managers should be included in or represented on the committee. These must include those who are able to answer for the likely safety, reliability, performance, cost and timescale consequences of changes, the effects on work in progress and the feasibility or otherwise of introducing the change into manufacture or construction.

In some cases, especially in projects involving the nuclear industry, aviation, defence or other cases where reliability, safety or performance assume great significance, two key members of the committee represent:

- the design authority (typically the chief engineer);
- the inspecting authority (a person such as a quality manager who should be independent and able to make assessments on the basis of quality alone, without commercial pressure).

Change committees often meet on a regular basis, dealing with change requests in batches. Others avoid meetings by circulating requests around the committee members, so that each member considers the effect of the proposed change on his or her area of responsibility.

Decision criteria

Points which have to be examined by the committee include the following:

- Is the change actually possible to make?
- Is it a customer-requested or a self-inflicted change?
- What is the estimated cost of the change?
- Will the customer pay? If so, what should be the price?
- If the change is not customer-requested, is it really necessary? Why?
- What will be the effect on progress?
- How will safety, reliability and performance be affected?
- If several identical sets of equipment are being produced, at

what point in the production sequence should the change be introduced?

- Will scrap or redundant materials be created?
- Are any items to be changed retrospectively? Are these:

  - in production or construction?
  - in stock?
  - already delivered to the customer?

- What drawings, specifications and other documents will have to be modified?

When the committee has considered all these questions, it has the following options:

- Authorize the change as requested.
- Give limited approval only, authorizing the change with specified limitations.
- Refer the request back to the originator (or elsewhere) asking for clarification or for an alternative solution.
- Reject the change, giving reasons.

Registration and progressing

In any project organization where changes are expected (which really means all project organizations) it is advisable to nominate a change coordinating clerk. This is not usually a full-time role, and the person chosen will probably carry out other clerical or administrative duties for the project. The change coordinating clerk may reside in a contracts office, the project manager's administration group, the engineering department or in some other place. His or her duties are likely to include:

- registering each change request and allocating a serial number to it;
- distributing and filing copies of the change documents;
- following up to ensure that every request is considered by the change committee without avoidable delay;
- distributing and filing copies of the change documents after the committee's instructions have been given; and

- following up to ensure that authorized changes are carried out and that all drawings and specifications affected by the change are updated and re-issued.

Change registers should be designed to highlight engineering change requests that are with the change committee for consideration or which are otherwise still 'active' and requiring monitoring to prevent delays. For example, a column can be provided on the register headed 'final issue date' or something similar. The absence of a date in that column tells the coordinator that the change is still active and in need of monitoring and progressing.

Formal procedures for external change requests

Changes requested by the customer which affect price, delivery or any other aspect of the original purchase order or contract require formal documentation. This documentation should fulfil the following functions:

- Describe the change.
- Amend the purchase order or contract.
- Authorize the contractor to make the change.
- Promise payment.
- Agree to any associated timescale revision.

Where the original contract was in the form of a purchase order, the customer will usually request a change by issuing a purchase order amendment. In other cases, especially for projects involving construction, changes are recorded on contract variation orders (sometimes called 'project variations' or 'contract variations'). An example is given in Figure 11.1. Similar changes arranged by a main contractor with site construction subcontractors are often known as site variation orders.

Commercial administration of customer changes

On a large project of long duration and of technical complexity, it is quite likely that many formal project variations and informal

Project variation order	PVO number:
	Project number:
Project title:	Issue date:

Summary of change (use continuation sheets if necessary):

Originator: Date:

Effect on project schedule:

Effect on costs and price: Cost estimate ref.:

Customer's authorization details: Our authorization:

Distribution:

Figure 11.1   Project variation

change requests will be received from the customer or client. Some of these changes might require a great deal of discussion before they can be agreed and implemented. There may even be occasions when customers will change their minds during the course of protracted negotiations about the technical and commercial details of a proposed change.

It is easy to appreciate that, as time proceeds, a very complicated situation can develop. There will be changes already agreed and implemented, others agreed but not yet implemented, some being negotiated and perhaps a few that are giving rise to argument or even dispute.

The way in which any individual case is handled is likely to be the responsibility of the contractor's commercial or contracts department (or the legal department if things start to get out of hand). However, the project manager has responsibility for achieving the project objectives and, obviously, has to keep track of what those objectives actually are. This can be difficult when the changes are many, complex and at different stages of agreement.

It is important, therefore, to maintain an up-to-date log of all these customer changes and to make certain that this accurately records their effect on the project specification, scope, budget and price. This task is often assigned to a cost engineer or to the person or group responsible for coordinating cost management and planning. It should be possible to consult the log at any time to identify the following:

- All changes requested by the customer up to the current time.
- The relevant contract variation or purchase order amendment number in every case.
- The status of each change, that is whether it has been:

  - agreed
  - priced (with details)
  - implemented
  - invoiced.

- The total current increase in project price resulting from changes that have been agreed with the customer.

In very complex cases, the change log will act as a file index for all the supporting records of meetings, correspondence and technical documents.

Very large sums of money, considerable time delays and matters of professional competence or liability can be bound up in all these changes. If a proper system for logging and progressing them is not put in place near the start of a project, the situation can easily become very confused, putting the contractor at serious commercial and legal risk.

Formal procedure for internal change requests

When a designer, in a fit of rage or despair, tears up a drawing or clears the computer screen and starts again, there is no need to invoke a formal change engineering procedure. Any new design might have to undergo many changes before it is committed to a fully checked and issued drawing. This is all part of the normal, creative development process. Provided that the design intentions remain within the requirements of the design specification, any internal changes made before drawings are formally issued are not generally considered to be modifications or engineering changes.

Some companies circulate early, pre-issue drawings for discussion, advance information or approval. These issues are often distinguished from the fully released versions by labelling them as revision A, revision B and so on, changing the revision numbers to the series 0, 1, 2 and so on to denote official releases. A rule might, therefore, be suggested that formal engineering change procedures need only be applied to drawing revisions made after the first issue for manufacturing or construction. But such a rule can fall apart if preliminary issues are made for the manufacture of a prototype, in which changes must be properly controlled.

Another reason for invoking formal procedures is found whenever there is an intention to depart from the design specification, especially when the development work is being carried out for an external customer. This, again, is a case for using the formal change procedure before any drawing has been issued for manufacture or construction.

Some rule or criterion is needed to determine at which point in the design process the formal change procedure should be introduced. The question to ask is 'Will the proposed change affect any instruction, specification, plan or budget that has already been agreed with other departments, the customer or other external organization?' If the answer to this question is 'Yes', the probability is that formal change committee approval will be needed.

Change request forms

Individuals should always put their change requests in writing to the change committee. A standard form should be used, designed in such a way that the originator is induced to answer in advance all the questions that the change committee will want to ask. An example is shown in Figure 11.2. Change requests of this type are used widely in engineering projects, although they may be known by different titles, invariably abbreviated to sets of initials. The following are among those which may be encountered:

ECR   Engineering change request
ECO   Engineering change order
MR   Modification request

The purpose of an engineering change request is to describe, document and seek formal permission for a permanent design change. The change may be unfunded or it might be the result of a contract variation order and, therefore, funded by the customer.

Any person should be allowed to originate an engineering change request, since it can have no effect until it has been authorized by the change committee. The method for completing the form should be self-evident from Figure 11.2.

Design freeze

Sometimes project organizations recognize that there is a point in the design and construction of a project after which any change would be particularly irksome, inconvenient or potentially damaging. This leads to the announcement of a design freeze, or the declaration of a 'stable design' condition, after which the change

Engineering change request		ECR number:
Project title:		Project number:

Details of change requested (use continuation sheets if necessary):

Drawings and other documents affected:

Reason for request:

Originator: Date:

Emergency action requested (if any):

Effect on costs: Cost estimate ref.:

Will customer pay, yes ☐   no ☐   If yes, customer authorization ref.:

Effect on project schedule?

COMMITTEE INSTRUCTIONS: CHANGE APPROVED ☐   NOT APPROVED ☐

Point of embodiment, stocks, work in progress, units in service, special restrictions, etc.:

Authorized by: Date:

Figure 11.2   Engineering change request

committee will refuse to consider any change request unless there are compelling reasons, such as safety or a customer request. Ideally the customer should agree to be bound by the design freeze.

The interchangeability rule

The usual practice when a drawing is changed is to re-issue it with a new revision number. If, however, a change results in a manufactured component or assembly being made different from other items with which it was previously interchangeable, it is not sufficient merely to change the drawing revision number. The drawing number itself (and therefore the part number) must also be changed.

This is a golden rule to which no exception should ever be allowed, whether the item is a small component or a big assembly.

Example

Suppose that a project requires the use of 1000 small spacers, and that after 500 had been produced in brass the design was cheapened to use mild steel. These spacers are truly interchangeable and the part number need not be changed. But the drawing for the steel spacers would have to be given a new revision number.

Now suppose that the design had been changed instead to moulded nylon because on some later manufactured assemblies it became necessary for the spacers to be electrically insulating. Because the metal spacers can no longer be used on all assemblies, the nylon spacers must be given a new distinguishing drawing and part number.

Emergency modifications

If the need for an essential, urgent modification is discovered, there may simply be no time available in which to follow the set change procedure rules and issue suitably changed drawings.

There are right and wrong ways of dealing with this situation and the following case history is a good, all too common, example of the latter.

Case history – the Kosy-Kwik Company

The project setting
Kosy-Kwik was a company which specialized in the design, supply and installation of heating and air-conditioning systems. In 1990 it was awarded a contract, as subcontractors to a large building group, to plan and install all the heating and ventilation arrangements in a new multi-storey office block commissioned by the Coverite Insurance Company Ltd. Two engineers, Clarke and Jackson, were assigned to the project. Whilst Clarke was given overall design responsibility, Jackson was detailed off to plan the central control panel and its associated controls and instrumentation.

Early difficulties
We join the project near the end of the preparation period in the Kosy-Kwik factory. By this time most deliveries of plant and equipment had been made to the Coverite premises, except for the control panel, which was still being fabricated, later than scheduled.

Jackson was a conscientious engineer who took a great interest in his jobs as they passed through the factory. He was in the habit of making periodical tours to keep a check on progress and the results of his design. It was during one of these tours that Jackson was approached by the sheet metal shop foreman. It appeared that the Coverite control panel, now welded together, was weak and wobbly.

Jackson could only agree with the foreman. The front panel was indeed decidedly flimsy, as a result of a glaring design error in specifying a gauge of steel that was far too thin. Delivery of this panel to site was already late and threatened to delay the whole project. There was simply no time available in which to start building a new control panel. In any case, the extra cost would have been unwelcome. A simpler solution had to be found – a rescue package in fact.

Marked-up drawings

The engineer asked the foreman to weld some suitably chunky pieces of channel iron to the rear face of the panel to stiffen it up. The foreman agreed, but was worried about passing the job through the inspection department without a drawing. 'No problem!' said Jackson, who took a pen from his pocket, marked up the foreman's copy of the drawing and signed it to authorize the alteration.

The modification was successful. Everyone concerned was very relieved, not least Jackson, whose reputation had been likely to suffer. Only a few hours were lost and the panel was duly delivered. The remainder of the project went ahead without further mishap and the Coverite Insurance Company Ltd joined the long list of Kosy-Kwik's satisfied customers.

The follow-up project

In the summer of 1995 Kosy-Kwik was awarded a follow-up contract by the Coverite Insurance Company. Its offices were to be extended, with a new wing to house computer services and staff. Coverite was working to a well-planned but tight schedule, which demanded that the new wing should be opened on the first working day of 1996. Because of the rigid timescale restrictions, several contract conditions were imposed on Kosy-Kwik. In particular, the only complete shutdown period allowed for the existing heating and ventilating plant (for connecting and testing the additional circuits and controls) was to be during the Christmas break. Otherwise the Coverite Company would suffer loss of work by its office staff. There was also a penalty payment of £400 for every week or part of a week by which Kosy-Kwik failed to meet the scheduled end date.

During the five years which separated these two projects several changes had occurred in the Kosy-Kwik organization. Clarke received a well-deserved promotion to a remote branch office, where he became area manager. Jackson retired to enjoy his pension. The engineering department expanded and attracted several new recruits. Among these was Stevens, an experienced contract engineer. He had no means of contact with Clarke or Jackson and was unlikely ever to meet either of them.

Preparation for the new project
Stevens was appointed as engineer in charge of the new Coverite project. He decided that the best policy would be to prefabricate as many parts of the project as possible in the factory. This would reduce the amount of work to be done on site and ensure that the final link-up and testing could be accomplished during the Christmas break. Stevens found a roll of drawings labelled 'Coverite Project' in a dead file drawer, dusted them off and set to work.

Most of the system was found to be straightforward, and the final tying-in with the existing installation was to be achieved by providing the installation engineers with a bolt-on package that could be fitted to the original control panel. This package was duly designed, manufactured and delivered to site along with all the other essential materials. By the time Christmas arrived, all equipment, pipes and ducts were in place in the new part of the building. All that remained was for the final installation team to arrive, shut down the plant, modify the control panel with the kit provided and then test and set up the whole system.

The installation attempt
Early on Christmas Eve, two Kosy-Kwik fitters were sent to shut down the plant and start work on the control panel. Their first job was to cut a large rectangular hole in an unused part of the original panel in order to fit the new package. A template had been provided for this purpose, which they now placed in position. When they started cutting, the engineers met unexpected resistance in the shape of several large channel iron ribs welded to the rear face of the panel. The engineers had come prepared only to tackle the thin sheet shown on the old drawings. It took them over two hours and many saw blades before the hole was finished. Then they found that the connections to the new control package were fouled by what remained of the channel iron. Worse still, the panel was now weak and wobbly again.

The two engineers were experienced and trained as skilled installation fitters, but were equipped neither materially nor mentally to deal with problems of this magnitude without help. They suffered an acute sense of frustration and isolation, although they found different (shorter) words with which to express their feelings.

A cry for help was indicated. Unfortunately, however, the

response to their impassioned telephone call to Kosy-Kwik head-quarters was less than satisfactory. Against the background accompaniment of a spirited office party they learned that all the senior engineering and management staff had already left to start their holiday. The operator wished the fitters a 'Merry Christmas' and suggested that they 'Have a nice day'. The two engineers interpreted these greetings as good advice, gave up and went home to start their unexpected holidays.

The extra cost
There is no need to dwell at length on the consequences of this case or to describe the scenes of anguish and recriminations back at headquarters in the New Year. A short summary of the additional cost items follows:

		£
1	Design and manufacture new control panel modification kit	3500
2	Cost of time wasted during first visit of the two fitters	250
3	Cost of repairing weakened panel, on site	180
4	Contract penalty clause, 4 weeks at £400 per week	1600
	Total additional costs, directly attributable	5530

Post-mortem
A retrospective glance at the circumstances which led to the disastrous consequences of the Coverite project will provide a useful basis for describing a more reliable method of dealing with very urgent modifications.

In this example, all troubles can be traced back to the use of a marked-up drawing on the sheet metal shop floor, the details of which were not passed back to the original project drawings. The use of marked-up drawings is generally to be deplored, but we have to be realistic about this problem and accept that there will be occasions when they are unavoidable, when there is simply no time in which to update the master drawings or computer file and issue new copies of the drawing. Under these circumstances, some sort of temporary documentation must suffice, but only where safeguards are in place to ensure that the original drawings do get changed to show the true 'as-built' condition of the project.

Safeguards

One way in which the updating of final drawings can be safe-guarded in the event of emergency changes relies on a stream-lined version of the formal modification procedure, without bypassing any of the important control points. The originator of the emergency modification must write out an engineering change request and get it registered by the change coordinator. After seeking the immediate approval of the chief engineer (or the nominated deputy), the originator must pass one copy to the design office in order that the change will eventually be incorporated in the drawings. Another copy of the change request is kept by the coordinating clerk, who must make certain that it is seen at the next change committee meeting. The original change request form is passed to the production department for action, where it becomes part of the issued manufacturing instructions.

If a working copy of a drawing does have to be marked up, which may be inevitable if there is insufficient space on the change request form, an identical marked up copy must be deposited in the design office, together with its copy of the change request. A photocopy is preferred for this purpose, to ensure that the dupli-cate is indeed a true copy, eliminating any possibility of clerical errors or omissions. The original change request must accompany the job right through all its production stages, particularly until it reaches final inspection and testing.

12

Managing progress

This chapter starts from the premise that an effective schedule has been produced, and that all key project participants know, and have willingly agreed to, what is expected of them.

Project progressing as a closed loop control system

Project progressing can be regarded as part of a closed loop control system. For every instruction which is sent out, the system response has to be monitored and a resulting feedback signal must be generated. Otherwise there will be no way of knowing when corrective actions are needed. The project manager will ensure that these corrective actions do take place, so that the control loop is closed. Figure 12.1 illustrates this concept.

Management by exception

With any system of control feedback, it is the errors that are significant, because it is the phase and amplitude of these that generate corrective action. In the management context these errors are called 'exceptions' and the sensible approach of concentrating reports and attention on such exceptions is known as 'management by exception'.

Management by surprise

There is an alternative management approach that relies only on outgoing instructions, with no feedback or error signals. This is called 'management by surprise', because the manager feeds in work at one end of the system and is surprised when it doesn't come out at the other!

Progress monitoring and schedule updating

Active projects depend on two-way communication between the project manager and every departmental manager. Work instructions must be issued and information must be fed back regularly on the resulting progress.

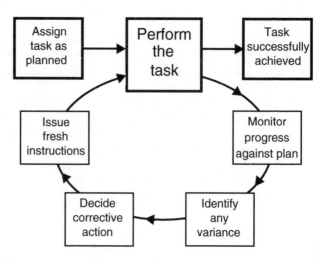

Figure 12.1   Control feedback loop for a project task

Use of work-to lists as progress returns

If the instructions are to be conveyed from the project manager to participants by way of work-to lists, there is no reason why the same procedure should not be applied in reverse to feed back progress information. The only missing item is a document complementary to the work-to list. This gap can be filled by:

- the use of specially designed progress return forms;
- line managers annotating and returning copies of their work-to lists; or
- direct input to the computer via a network.

The first option introduces more forms and clerical work, which should obviously be avoided if possible.

For the second option, Open Plan is one software package which has a combined work-to list and questionnaire report in its standard range of reports (see Figure 12.2). Other packages also allow space for comments on their work-to lists or task lists.

For the last option, it is often practicable for departmental managers to be given direct access to the computer files through their own terminals. These managers can then report progress by this direct, 'real time' method. The project manager will want to be assured that progress information fed directly to the computer in this way, without first being subjected to checking and critical examination, emanates only from reliable and reasonably senior staff. False input statements could lead to subsequent errors in network analysis, resource scheduling and future work-to lists. If the computer is holding a large, complex multiproject model, the group or person responsible for scheduling will always be wary of any input that could corrupt the files and cause many hours of restoration work.

Although project progress information will be updated continuously by the direct input method, the work-to lists and other schedules will probably only be revised and re-issued when the planner decides that data reprocessing is necessary. This decision must be made by the planner in advance, and the next 'time-now' date (see below) must be announced as soon as it is decided.

Project: Garage

GARAGE PROJECT
Activity progress update questionnaire

ID	Description	Orig dur	Scheduled start	Scheduled finish	Rem dur	% comp	% complete	Progress at next time now / Comment
1	Project start	0	13MAY02	13MAY02	0	0		
2	Make and prime door frame	1	13MAY02	13MAY02	1	0		
3	Dig foundations	4	13MAY02	16MAY02	4	0		
7	Position door frame	1	14MAY02	14MAY02	1	0		
4	Make doors	3	15MAY02	17MAY02	3	0		
8	Concrete foundations	2	17MAY02	20MAY02	2	0		
9	Prime doors	1	20MAY02	20MAY02	1	0		
11	Lay bricks for walls	10	21MAY02	03JUN02	10	0		
13	Fit RSJ lintel	1	04JUN02	04JUN02	1	0		
18	Case lintel, build parapets	2	05JUN02	06JUN02	2	0		
12	Lay floor base	2	07JUN02	10JUN02	2	0		

Figure 12.2 Combined work-to list and progress questionnaire

Frequency of progress data collection

Progress feedback should be arranged at fairly frequent intervals, typically more often than the issue of revised work-to lists. If the intervals are too long, some problems might not come to light in sufficient time for corrective action.

Time-now date

All progress data should be given with reference to the next 'time-now' date, which is the date chosen to act as a reference point from which time analysis and rescheduling will be calculated when the computer schedule is updated.

All people asked to provide progress information, whether direct from terminals or on paper, must be told the next time-now date as far in advance as possible. The planner will usually choose this time-now to be either the date on which rescheduling is to take place or a few days later.

If the schedules have to be updated frequently, as a result of changes or for any other reason, reprocessing might have to be arranged at regular intervals. If the intervals are regular, the rescheduling dates and time-now dates can be announced and annotated on calendars for many months ahead.

Quality and reliability of progress information

Whatever the method used for progress feedback, care must be taken to avoid either ambiguity or undue complication. The simpler the method, the more likely will be the chances of persuading all the managers involved to return data regularly on time. Even so, training all key participants to adopt the regular routine of progress reporting often provides project managers with a real test of their mettle. Many attempts at project control break down because this particular process cannot be reliably established.

Nature of information for updating computer schedules

Whether the system's progress input starts from a paper questionnaire or direct keyboard intervention by line managers, the following facts or estimates are usually required for each activity that has been started, finished or worked on since the previous report or keyboard visit:

- If started since the previous report, what was the actual starting date?
- If started but not finished, either:
  - the estimated percentage completion at time-now; or
  - the estimated remaining duration after time-now.
- Is the activity finished?
- If finished, what was the actual finish date?

Questions of logic

If the progress information is being gathered on forms, rather than by keyed input, there is another question that the perceptive project manager needs to ask for each task reported as complete. The vital question is *Can this activity's immediate successor(s) be started?* This question (not usually asked or possible to answer when progress information is being keyed into the computer) is the acid test of whether or not an activity has truly been completed. If the network logic is correct, then an activity cannot strictly be reported as complete if its immediately following dependent tasks cannot be started.

An alert project manager will recognize the danger behind a progress return which says that the percentage progress achieved is 99 or 100 per cent, but that the next activity cannot start. This could mean that the progress claimed has not in fact been made. This anomaly also occurs when a design engineer has completed a batch of drawings, but refuses to release them for issue through lack of confidence in the design, or because he or she feels that (given plenty of time) the drawings could be made more perfect, or for some other non-essential personal reason.

Sometimes an activity can be started even though one or more of its predecessors is still in progress. For example, an activity, although not complete, could be sufficiently advanced to allow the release of procurement lists for long-lead items. A network diagram may not always indicate such possibilities and very often these opportunities for expediting progress would be missed by individuals who had not regularly asked the right questions.

Activities are quite often reported as started before one or more predecessors have been reported as finished. This is in contradiction to the logic enshrined in the network so when it happens it indicates that the network constraints were not absolute. None the less, if that is the situation, then it has to be accepted and reported to the computer accordingly: most software should be capable of accepting 'out of sequence' progress data.

Management by walkabout

The routine methods described above for collecting progress information can work properly only in an ideal world. They paint a picture of the project manager working entirely from behind a desk, issuing instructions and receiving reports while the project proceeds smoothly on to its successful finish. While the establishment of efficient routine systems is a commendable and necessary aim, more is needed. The project manager must be prepared to depart from the routine and his or her desk from time to time, making visits and spot checks, giving praise or encouragement where due and viewing physical progress at first hand. This process is sometimes called 'management by walkabout'.

Visits to sites or production areas are particularly useful when two or more visits are made some little time apart, so that progress (or lack of it) can be noted. Construction site photographs should be taken on such visits, for checking progress and as a permanent record of the project as it develops.

Statistical checks

One very useful occasional check is to ask how many people in a department or of a particular grade are actually working on the project. The answer can then be compared with the manpower planned for that date. Comparison of scheduled and actual cost curves can also be made, but the head count is quicker, more positive, and likely to produce the earlier warning.

Suppose that 35 design engineers are supposed to be working on scheduled activities on a given date. If only 18 people can be counted, something is obviously very wrong somewhere. Although routine progress returns might indicate that everything is more or less on course, the 'head count' shows that work on the project in the design department is not taking place at the required rate.

When action is taken, it may be found that the project design is held up for lack of information, that other work has been given priority or that the department is seriously under-staffed. The project manager must investigate the reason and take steps to set the right number of people to work.

When the news is bad

How bad?

When jobs start to run late, the first thing that the project manager must do is to consider the possible effects on:

● the current project;
● projects or other work queuing in the pipeline; and
● the customer.

On rare occasions, late running might be acceptable and require no action. Usually, however, some degree of corrective action is needed. The project manager must then assess the situation, decide the appropriate action and implement it.

Jobs with free float
If the recalcitrant task has enough free float to absorb the delay, then all that needs to be done is to expedite the work and finish it without further interruption, within the available free float.

Jobs with some total float
Total float has to be treated with more circumspection than free float, because any total float used up by late working early in the programme will rob later tasks of their float. So, those jobs which possess total float but no free float should, wherever possible, be expedited to bring them back on schedule.

Remember that purchasing and manufacturing departments have always suffered at the hands of project managers by being expected to perform miracles when all the total float has been used up long before work enters the purchasing and manufacturing phases.

Jobs with zero or negative float

If critical tasks (tasks with zero or negative float) are late, then special measures must certainly be taken. It might be necessary to accept more expensive working methods to expedite these late jobs and bring them back on schedule. If a task expected to cost £1000 is in danger of running several weeks late and jeopardizing the handover date of a project worth £1m, then obviously it would be worth spending £10000 or even more on the problem task if that could rescue the complete programme. The project manager must always view the costs of expediting individual activities against the benefits gained for the whole project.

Corrective measures

Corrective measures will only be successful if they are taken in time, which means that adequate warning of problems must be given. This will depend on having a well-prepared schedule, keeping it up to date and monitoring progress regularly.

Working overtime, perhaps over one or two weekends, can sometimes recover time. The project manager will be relieved, on such occasions, that overtime working was not built into the normal schedules as customary practice. Used occasionally, overtime can be helpful in overcoming delays. Used regularly or too often, however, the law of diminishing returns will apply, with staff permanently tired and working under pressure, and with no adequate reserves to cope with emergencies.

If problems are being caused by shortage of resources, perhaps these could be made available from external sources by subcontracting. Or, there might be additional capacity elsewhere in the contractor's organization that could be mobilized.

The network logic should always be re-examined critically. Can some tasks be overlapped, bypassed or even eliminated?

Special motivational measures, incentives or even unorthodox actions can sometimes give progress a much needed boost, provided that these measures are not repeated too often and are used sensibly.

Progress meetings

Any project manager worthy of the title will want to make certain that whenever possible his or her tactics are preventive rather than curative. If a special meeting can be successful in resolving problems, why not pre-empt trouble by holding regular progress meetings, with senior representatives of all departments present?

Regular progress meetings provide a suitable forum where two-way communication can take place between planners and participants. The main purposes of progress meetings emerge as a means of keeping a periodic check on the project progress, and the making of any decisions to implement corrective action if programme slippages occur or appear likely.

Frequency

The frequency with which meetings are held must depend to a large extent on the nature of the project, the size and geographical spread of its organization and its timescale.

On projects of short duration, and with much detail to be considered, there may be a good case for holding progress meetings frequently, say once a week, on an informal basis at supervisor level. For other projects monthly meetings may be adequate. Meetings at relatively junior level can be backed up by less frequent meetings held at more senior level. Project review meetings, which can cover the financial prospects as well as simple progress, can also be arranged: the company's general manager may wish to attend such meetings and for some capital projects the customer might also want to be represented.

Meetings held more frequently than necessary create apathy or hostility. Departmental supervisors and managers are usually busy people whose time should not be wasted.

Keeping to the subject

There are certain dangers associated with the mismanagement of progress meetings. For instance, lengthy discussions often arise between two specialists on technical issues that should be resolved outside the meeting. Such discussions can bore the other members of the meeting, waste their scarce and expensive time and cause rapid loss of interest in the proceedings. Although it is never possible to divorce technical considerations from progress topics, design meetings and progress meetings are basically different functions which should be kept apart. Discussions should be kept to key progress topics, with irrelevancies swept aside.

Was the meeting successful?

When a meeting breaks up, it will have been successful only if all the members feel that they have achieved some genuine purpose and that actions have been agreed which will benefit the project. Demands made of members during the meeting must be achievable, so that promises extracted can be honoured.

Issuing the minutes

The minutes must be published without delay so that they do not become outdated by further events before distribution. Minutes should be clearly and concisely written, combining brevity with clarity, accuracy and careful layout, so that each action demanded can be seen to stand out from the page. If the document is too bulky it may not even be read by everyone. Short, pointed statements of fact are all that is required.

No ambiguity must be allowed after any statement as to who is directly responsible for taking action. Every person listed for taking action must receive a copy of the minutes (although this sounds obvious, the point is sometimes overlooked). Times must be stated definitively. Expressions such as 'at the end of next week' or 'towards the end of the month' should be avoided in favour of actual dates.

Progress meetings abandoned

The above account of progress meetings adheres to the conventional view that progress meetings are an accepted way of project life. Here is some food for less conventional thought.

A heavy engineering company had long been accustomed to holding progress meetings. Depending on the particular project manager, these were held either at regular intervals or randomly whenever things looked like going badly adrift (most readers will have encountered such 'firefighting' meetings). Several projects were in progress at any one time, and the permanent engineering department of about 60 people was often augmented by as many as 80 subcontracted staff working either in-house or in external offices.

Meetings typically resulted in a set of excuses from participants as to why actions requested of them at previous meetings had been carried out late, ineffectually or not at all. Each meeting would end with a new set of promises, ready to fuel a fresh collection of excuses at the next meeting. This is not to say that the company's record was particularly bad, but there was considerable room for improvement and too much time was being wasted at too many meetings.

Senior company management, recognizing the problem, supported a study which led to the introduction of critical path network planning for all projects, using a computer to schedule resources and issue detailed work-to lists. Two progress engineers were engaged, one to follow up in-house work and the other to supervise outside subcontractors. Both engineers had the benefit of the work-to lists, which told them exactly which jobs should be in progress at any time, the scheduled start and finish dates for these jobs, how many people should be working on each of them, how many people should be working in total on each project at any time and the amount of float left for every activity.

By following up activities on a day-by-day basis from the work-to lists, these two progress engineers succeeded in achieving a considerable improvement in progress and the smooth flow of work. If a critical or near-critical activity looked like running late, stops were pulled out to bring it back into line (by working overtime during evenings and weekends if necessary). Fortunately, all the staff were cooperative, grateful (in fact) for the new sense of order created in their working lives.

After several months under this new system it dawned on all the company managers that they were no longer being asked to attend progress meetings. Except for kick-off meetings at the introduction of new projects, progress meetings had become redundant.

Project progress reports

Internal reports to company management

Progress reports addressed to company management will have to set out the technical, fulfilment and financial status of the project and compare the company's performance in each of these respects with the scheduled requirements. For projects lasting more than a few months, such reports are usually issued at regular intervals, and they may well be presented by the project manager during the course of project review meetings.

Discussion of a report might trigger important management decisions that could lead to changes in contract policy or project organization. For these and many other reasons it is important that data relevant to the condition and management of the project are presented factually, supported where necessary by carefully reasoned predictions or explanations.

These reports may contain detailed information of a proprietary nature. They might, therefore, have to be treated as confidential, with their distribution restricted to a limited number of people, all within the company management.

Exception reports

There is another type of internal management report in addition to the detailed management reports just described. These are the reports of 'exceptions' and are confined in scope to those project factors which are giving rise to acute concern and which must receive immediate attention if the project is to be held on course. If the report is to do with costs, the exceptions will probably be listed as 'variances', but variances are so-called whether they are adverse or advantageous divergences from plan.

Exception reports can be contained in documents such as adverse cost reports, materials shortage lists or computer print-outs of jobs running late. At the other extreme, an exception report might be the frenzied beating on a senior manager's door by a distraught project manager who feels that his project and his world have suddenly fallen apart.

Before allowing any exception report to be passed to more senior management, the project manager must first be certain that some remedy within his or her own control cannot be found. Once it has been established that events are likely to move out of control, however, the project manager has a clear duty to appraise senior management of the facts without delay.

All of this is, of course, following the sensible practice of 'management by exception'. This seeks to prevent senior managers from being bombarded with large volumes of routine information which should be of concern only to supervisors and junior managers. The intention is to leave executive minds free to concentrate their efforts where they can be employed to the best advantage of the company and its projects.

Reports to the client or customer

The submission of formal progress reports to the client or customer could be one of the conditions of contract. If the customer does expect regular reports then, quite obviously, these can be derived from the same source which compiled all the data and explanations for the internal management reports. Some of the more detailed technical information in the internal reports may not be of interest to the customer or relevant to its needs. Customer progress reports, therefore, are to some extent edited versions of internal management reports.

Whether or not financial reports of any type are to be bound in or attached to customers' progress reports will depend on the main contractor's role in each case. Under some circumstances cost and profitability predictions must be regarded as proprietary information, not to be disclosed outside the company. In other cases, the project manager may have to submit cost summaries or more detailed breakdowns and forecasts.

Although customer reports may have to be edited in order to improve clarity and remove proprietary information, they must never intentionally mislead. It is always best to keep the customer informed of the true progress position, especially when slippages have occurred which cannot be contained within the available float. Any attempt to put off the evil day by placating a customer with optimistic forecasts or unfounded promises must lead to unwelcome repercussions eventually. Nobody likes to discover that they have been deceived, and customers are no exception to this rule.

Project closure

Project closure document

Just as a formal document of authority has to be issued to open a project and allow expenditure to begin, so the end of a project should be marked by a formal announcement. The formal closure notice need only be a very simple form, but it should include the following:

- Project title.
- Project number.
- The effective closure date.
- Reason for closure (usually, but not always, because the project has been finished).
- Any special instructions.
- Closure authorization signature.
- Distribution, which should at least include all those who received the authorization notice when the project was opened.

An example of a project closure notice is given in Figure 12.3. This contains more details than those listed above, including a checklist of closedown activities. The checklist is primarily concerned with the final updating and retention of project documents, to ensure that:

- the final as-built condition of the project is properly defined; and
- all documents which could have subsequent commercial or legal liability significance are properly identified and retained.

Cost cut-off

The most usual reason for issuing a formal project closure statement is to forbid further expenditure against the main project cost codes. This is particularly important if hard-won profits are not to be eroded by an insidious continuation of time sheet bookings to the project simply because the account still happens to be open.

Notice of project closure

The following project will be closed to time bookings and all expenses with effect from the date given below

Client: Lox Chemicals Limited   Project number: LX 5150

Project title: Loxylene Plant (Huddersfield)   Closure date: 20 Apr 01

The following budgets are hereby authorized for the closedown activities marked in the checklist below

Department	Man-hours by standard cost staff grade						£
	1	2	3	4	5	6	
Project engineering	10			20	40		960
Planning				10			140
Purchasing			15				240
Installation and commissioning							
Construction management	5						100
Computing				1			14
Records and archives			10		200		2560
TOTALS	15		25	31	240		4014

Special instructions:
     Take special care with filing. A follow-up project is expected.
     All files to be destroyed after five years unless otherwise
     directed below.

CHECKLIST OF PROJECT CLOSURE ACTIVITIES

Project case history	PM to write, keep it brief
Project specification	Has been kept up to date but needs checking
Project variations	List and check that the file is complete
Drawing schedules	Keep 10 years in engineering files
Design calculations	Keep indefinitely in engineering files
Our drawings	Check they are as-built and keep indefinitely
Client's drawings	Return to client
Purchase control schedules	Keep 10 years in engineering files
Vendors' drawings	Keep 10 years
Purchase orders	
Expediting/inspection reports	
Test certificates	Keep 10 years
Operating/maintenance instructions	Keep 15 years
Spares lists	
Maintenance contracts	
Subcontract documents	Keep 10 years
Correspondence files	
Final cost records	Keep 10 years in general reference files
Photographs	Edit. Discuss with publicity dept and client
Critical path networks	Destroy after 1 year and erase computer files
Management information system	Delete project from MIS at year end

Prepared by: A.Scribe   Project manager: I. Diddit   Authorized by: *B. J. G. Whitechief*

Figure 12.3   Project closure notice, with checklist

It is well known that the recording of man-hours on time sheets is open to abuse; there is always a tendency for the less scrupulous staff to try and 'lose' unaccountable time by booking it to large projects where, it is hoped, it will go unnoticed. Obviously, good supervision will minimize this risk, but an instruction to the computer to reject all further time sheet entries against the project number is more effective.

Company accountants may wish to hold a project account open for their own use beyond the official project closure date to collect a few 'tail-end' costs. Although further man-hour time bookings are banned after the closure date, there are usually items such as late invoices from suppliers and subcontractors. On a large project these can continue to arrive for several months after project completion. They can represent considerable sums, but they should not affect the calculated profit significantly because (unless there has been loose control of subcontracts and dayworks) these costs should have been known and accrued in the accounts when they were committed (that is, when the orders were issued).

If costs are expected against the activities listed in the project closure checklist, these can be authorized and controlled by opening a new project for the purpose, with strictly limited budgets and with only nominated personnel able to book to the project on time sheets.

Select bibliography

Association of Cost Engineers (1991), *Estimating Checklist for Capital Projects*, 2nd edn, London, Spon

Baguley, Philip (1999), *Project Management*, London, Teach Yourself Books

Baily, P. (1991), *Purchasing Systems and Records*, 3rd edn, Aldershot, Gower

Burke, Rory (1999), *Project Management: Planning and Control*, 3rd edn, Chichester, Wiley

Chapman, C. B. and Ward, S. A. (1996), *Project Risk Management Processes, Techniques and Insights*, Chichester, Wiley

Churchouse, Chris (1999), *Managing Projects: A Gower Workbook*, Aldershot, Gower

Cleland, D. I. (ed.) (1998), *Field Guide to Project Management*, New York, Van Nostrand Reinhold

Cleland, D. I. and King, W. R. (1998), *Project Management Handbook*, 2nd edn, New York, Van Nostrand Reinhold

Croner's Reference Book for Exporters, Kingston-upon-Thames, Croner Publications (by subscription, updated monthly)

Croner's Reference Book for Importers, Kingston-upon-Thames, Croner Publications (by subscription, updated monthly)

Devaux, S. A. (1999), *Total Project Control: A Manager's Guide to Integrated Project Planning, Measuring and Tracking*, New York, Wiley

Farmer, D. and van Weele, A. J. (eds) (1995), *Gower Handbook of Purchasing Management*, 2nd edn, Aldershot, Gower

Grey, S. (1995), *Practical Risk Assessments for Project Management*, Chichester, Wiley

Hamilton, A. (1997), *Management by Projects*, London, Thomas Telford

Harrison, F. L. (1992), *Advanced Project Management: A Structured Approach*, 3rd edn, Aldershot, Gower

Hartman, Francis T. (2000), *Don't Park Your Brain Outside*, Penn. USA, Project Management Institute, Inc

Healey, P. L. (1997), *Project Management: Getting the Job Done on Time and in Budget*, Oxford, Butterworth-Heinemann

ICC (1990), *Incoterms 1990*, ICC Publication 460, International Chamber of Commerce, Paris (also available from ICC National Committees throughout the world)

Kerzner, H. (1997), *Project Management: A Systems Approach to Planning, Scheduling and Controlling*, 6th edn, New York, Van Nostrand Reinhold

Kliem, R. L. and Ludin, I. S. (1992), *The People Side of Project Management*, Aldershot, Gower

Kliem, Ralph L. and Ludin, Irwin S. (1993), *The Noah Project: The Secrets of Practical Project Management*, Aldershot, Gower

Lock, Dennis (2000), *Project Management*, 7th edn, Aldershot, Gower

Lockyer, K. G. and Gordon, J. (1996), *Critical Path Analysis and Other Project Management Techniques*, 6th edn, London, Pitman

Marsh, P. D. V. (2000), *Contracting for Engineering and Construction Projects*, 5th edn, Aldershot, Gower

Maylor, Harvey (1999), *Project Management*, 2nd edn, London, Pitman

Meredith, J. R. and Mantel, S. J. Jr (2000), *Project Management: A Managerial Approach*, 4th edn, New York, Wiley

Morris, P. W. G. (1997), *The Management of Projects*, London, Thomas Telford (principally a historical survey of project management, with extensive references)

Raftery, J. (1993), *Risk Analysis in Project Management*, London, Spon

Reiss, Geoff (1995), *Project Management Demystified: Today's Tools and Techniques*, 2nd edn, London, Spon

Reiss, Geoff (1996), *Programme Management Demystified: Managing Multiple Projects Successfully*, London, Spon

Shtub, A. and Bard, J. F. (1993), *Project Management: Engineering, Technology and Implementation*, Hemel Hempstead, Prentice-Hall

Smith, N. J. (1995), *Project Cost Estimating*, London, Thomas Telford

Turner, Rodney (1998), *Handbook of Project-based Management: Improving the Process for Achieving Strategic Objectives*, 2nd edn, Maidenhead, McGraw-Hill

Turner, Rodney and Simister, Stephen (eds), *Gower Handbook of Project Management*, 3rd edn, Aldershot, Gower

Wearne, S. H. (1989), *Control of Engineering Projects*, London, Thomas Telford

Woodward, J. F. (1997), *Construction Project Management: Getting it Right First Time*, London, Thomas Telford

Index